Bonjour
John et bonne année !!!
Voici de quoi t'inspirer
pour donner à ta cuisine des
airs de Provence !

A très bientôt ! :?
Chloé

(livre
choisi
par Chloé)
bises !

Je vous souhaite une bonne et heureuse
année 2016
à vous deux !
Ci joint un joli livre
de cuisine provençale, de
façon à ce que tu puisses
t'entraîner aux fourneaux,
car on vous attend cet été
à Espanon, avec les Dempsey
Je vous embrasse Véronique

LUNCH IN

PROVENCE

RACHAEL McKENNA
&
JEAN-ANDRÉ CHARIAL
OF OUSTAU DE BAUMANIÈRE

with an introduction by
PATRICIA WELLS

Flammarion

CONTENTS

INTRODUCTION
Patricia Wells

These are some of the snapshots I remember most clearly from the decades of my own lunches in Provence:

Sitting on our west-facing "sunset" terrace one afternoon in July, surrounded by good friends, with honey bees passing above, visiting the purple butterfly bush one moment, the lavender in bloom the next. We were grateful that the pesky mistral wind was not blowing, but rather a slight breeze from the east brushed our cheeks ever so gently. The sky was blue as blue can be, and the light had that impressionist's glow. We feasted on my friend Rolando's creation of the day, a dish we call Provence on a Plate, a colorful layered affair of fresh-from-the-garden eggplant, black olive tapenade from home-cured olives, heirloom tomatoes in red, yellow, and green, and a thin layer of local fresh goat's-milk cheese, all garnished with tender leaves of fresh basil. Homemade sourdough multigrain bread came from the wood-fired bread oven that morning, and our peppery red Côtes du Rhône, carefully decanted, joined us through the long and languid lunch. Best of all, there was the sound of laughter and good times, friendships were strengthened, and we knew that if these moments did not exist, we might try to make them up. Though not at all planned, that lunch lasted until six o'clock in the evening. That's just how grand lunch in Provence can be!

Joining a quartet of friends for a late August feast on the magical terrace of Oustau de Baumanière, about an hour's drive south of our farm. A sip of champagne rosé to celebrate Jeffrey's fiftieth birthday, then a late summer's palate of seasonal treats: an avalanche of summer vegetables—round zucchini crushed with toasted cumin, multicolored tomatoes, baby broad beans—all bathed in a warm, forward-flavored vegetable bouillon. We knew that many of the vegetables were just moments old, harvested that morning from owner Jean-André Charial's *potager*. The dappled light created a magical luminescence as the craggy hills of Les Baux formed a sturdy, comforting backdrop. We sipped Domaine Tempier's Bandol rosé and savored chef Sylvestre Wahid's Saint Pierre, that magnificent, firm-fleshed white fish from the Mediterranean, steamed on a mattress of fresh verdant seaweed, paired with baby squid cannellonis and a fine ratatouille, all manner of summer vegetables stewed separately to perfection. The chef's favored lamb chops and *filet*—from lamb that graze in the Auvergne in central France—were rubbed with spicy *ras el hanout* (the Middle Eastern blend of more than a dozen spices), teamed up with chickpeas, cumin, and a refreshing salad of fresh mint. Our winemaker's sturdy red wine, his top *cuvée* Gigondas—Santa Duc Hautes Garrigues—tasted right at home here, an afternoon that blended luxury, simplicity, perfection, and made for memories that would be cherished through the long winter.

All the possibilities are there: the freshest of fish and shellfish from the Mediterranean, fruits and vegetables from nearby farms and markets, wines from vineyards that hug the Rhône River valley, breads made from locally grown and ground épeautre (poor-man's-wheat), which grows so happily in the hills outside Nyons, lamb that grazes on the sides of Mont Ventoux.

Back on our terrace in Provence. An annual lunch with friends and their children. This time, remarkably, eight eight-year-old boys with hearty, open appetites joined us at the table for twenty. We sat on the east terrace beneath the centuries-old live oak tree with its crystal-clear view of Mont Ventoux, the highest peak in Provence. On the menu, as it often is, was my summer *soupe au pistou*, a signature vegetable soup that stars the fresh, creamy-white *coco blanc* shell beans, with understudies of red heirloom tomatoes, slim leeks, firm and tender carrots, potatoes, cubes of garden-fresh pumpkin or *potimarron*, tiny *haricots verts* or green beans, plump cloves of local garlic, and onions, embellished with a garden-fresh basil *sauce au pistou,* prepared with the sharp and peppery, tiny-leafed *basilic marseillais* traditionally used to prepare the sauce. The boys ate heartily and happily, until a local dog ran past with a live rabbit in its mouth. We rescued the rabbit and, at the insistence of one of the young boys, we placed him in a box to make him feel safe and secure, and fed him "lettuce, no vinaigrette." Family time, rich and well spent.

As *Lunch in Provence* so clearly conveys, the ritual experience is all about friends, fresh ingredients, sun, sky, and moments that build memories. It's not much about dining alone, though I could actually imagine a tranquil solitary lunch at a café, or a picnic savored on the top of a mountain after a long morning's hike. The meal need not be grand but the experience can surely be.

All the possibilities are there: the freshest of fish and shellfish from the Mediterranean, fruits and vegetables from nearby farms and markets, wines from vineyards that hug the Rhône River valley, breads made from locally grown and ground *épeautre* (poor-man's-wheat), which grows so happily in the hills outside Nyons, lamb that grazes on the sides of Mont Ventoux. Add to this recipe friends, sunshine, the great outdoors, and you have a good chance of creating an unforgettable experience. I have a friend from Washington, D.C., who framed a portrait of himself, smiling and well fed, seated at the outdoor café of the town square in the village of Villedieu (which translates as "God's town"). He had just enjoyed a generous onion, tomato, cheese, and black olive pizza from the pizza truck Chez Mumu parked on the square. My friend keeps the picture on his office desktop and looks at it all year long, and in his soul the memory of that moment is engraved, always to be his own.

The meal need not be grand but the experience can surely be.

Lunch in Provence should almost always be preceded by a morning visit to one of the region's outdoor markets—open-air festivals that take place weekly. In our town of Vaison-la-Romaine, I anticipate the Tuesday market day as if it were Christmas morning. Hundreds of merchants stream into the village before 6 a.m., setting up market stalls that will offer the freshest seasonal produce. Come summer we'll find shiny purple eggplant; all manner, color, shape, and size of heirloom tomatoes; sleek and firm zucchini in hues of green and yellow; mountains of summer salad greens, ranging from pungent arugula or *roquette* to the local multicolored salad mix known as *mesclun*. For lunch, there is always an endless shopping list of prepared foods: olive and pork sausage from the local butcher, a crispy rotisserie chicken, fresh spring rolls and tiny fried nems from the local Loatian, all manner of fresh goat's-milk cheese from the varied farm stands, and fresh Mediterranean anchovies and sardines ready for a quick cure of local extra-virgin olive oil and coarse sea salt for an instant first course accompanied by a sip of icy, chilled, and refreshing rosé wine. One's eyes are almost always bigger than one's stomach and, inevitably, we always end up with way too much food. But all these can go into a quickly concocted lunch in Provence, eaten alone or in tandem, savored in the welcoming outdoors.

My very first lunch in the South of France—a picnic by a cooling stream in some quiet corner of the Drôme—followed not a market visit but a marketing visit. We'd been invited for a long weekend in that rugged *département* to get away from the kinds of city pressures that had trailed us from New York to Paris. It's very hard to imagine feeling a need to flee Paris, but apparently we did.

Our hosts knew of a farm on the southern edge of that *département,* the area known as the Drôme Provençale, where the owners cured the tangy black Nyons olives harvested from their own trees, made an array of fruit *confitures* and jellies, and produced a full selection of honeys. There was also a hearty, heady *vin de pays* (regional wine) from the property. We were interested in the full bounty.

But buying meant sampling first. We sat on the terrace with the owner and his wife, tasting their olives, sampling the goat's-milk cheese that she sold at the festive markets in nearby villages, and, of course, trying their wine. It was a captivating moment—truly, because a short time later we bought our own Provençal farmhouse with a vineyard and olive and fruit trees. And now beehives, too.

A most recent, surprise lunch in Provence came as my students and I were preparing the midday feast, the final Friday celebration of the last week's class of the year. The week was glorious, with perfect weather, the grape harvest was on, and students were all eager and well-trained home cooks. That morning, we picked tiny, purple Ronde de Bordeaux figs and transformed them into a colorful tart, layering the pastry with a coating of almond paste made from local organic almonds, then cutting an "X" in the top of each fig and gently squeezing them open from the bottom so they looked like an elegant flower. We arranged them cut-side up on the almond mixture and baked them to bubbly perfection. A trio of students

The ritual experience is all about friends, fresh ingredients, sun, sky, and moments that build memories.

worked on the garden-fresh eggplants, roasted then cooked in a spicy tomato sauce. Another group transformed tiny, local, steamed *ratte* potatoes into a puckery salad laced with home-cured capers and *cornichons* (pickles or gherkins) and the small white Provençal onions known as *cébettes*. We fashioned a sorbet from yogurt, lemon zest, and honey from the hives on our farm. We hadn't ventured into the *potager* all morning, but when I decided that we needed a platter of sliced heirloom tomatoes and a tangle of greens for a salad, I sent a student out with a basket and scissors to harvest them. A huge squeal followed a minute later as she raced back into the house. In the middle of the previous night, a troupe of *sanglier*, or wild boar, had almost completely destroyed the vegetable garden, ripping out parsley, upturning perennial red and green sorrel plants, and leaving giant teeth marks on the pumpkins as well as zucchini. They didn't touch the tomatoes, ignored the arugula, and sniffed about the red and green *shiso* plants but didn't sample.

We took lots of photos, commiserated in the fact that this was the end of the season, not the peak, and knew that in a few days we'd be leaving Provence for Paris. It was a humorous and fitting end to the class—the last lunch in Provence of the season.

In Provence, we have the chance—not the promise—of dining outdoors at lunchtime 365 days a year. Even in the winter months of November through March, the blazing sun might decide to shine warm and bright, and that's when we happily take out our crisp, white, monogrammed linens, ceramic knife rests, silver cutlery, and fine wine glasses, and construct a culinary celebration. The meal may be simple but the pleasure grand, with a local farm chicken, roasted in the bread oven, anointed with a mild olive oil from the ripe and wrinkled *tanche* variety of olives from nearby Nyons. A wintry fennel and tomato stew will go with it, along with a trio of local goat's-milk cheeses from our local cheesemonger. Dessert might be a seasonal fruit, a few bunches of grapes that have been left on the vines after harvest, some welcoming tart Corsican clementines, or a fig purée—simmered and preserved in August—topped with a *fromage blanc* (white cheese) sorbet.

I remember one totally remarkable February day during one of my special black truffle cooking classes. It was so warm and sunny we moved the tables out on to the center of the terrace to make the best of the winter's warmth. We had just returned from a morning's truffle hunt with a dog named Dynamo. We donned straw hats and baseball caps and feasted on fresh black truffle *tartines*—open-faced truffle sandwiches on toasted homemade *brioche*; pumpkin soup with truffle cream, curry, and pumpkin seed oil; and finished with a truffle Chaource, the creamy cow's-milk cheese from the Champagne region to the north. Three days earlier I had sliced the cheese into layers like a wedding cake, slipped paper-thin discs of fresh black truffles between each layer, reconstructed the cheese, wrapped it tightly in plastic wrap and let it ripen and mature in the refrigerator. Yes, the same lunch could have been appreciated in the dining room in front of a roaring fire, yet the unanticipated surprise of the February sun added an additional note of drama, pleasure, satisfaction.

In Provence, we have the chance of dining outdoors at lunchtime 365 days a year … that's when we happily take out our crisp, white, monogrammed linens, ceramic knife rests, silver cutlery, and fine wine glasses, and construct a culinary celebration.

Of course, an indoor lunch in Provence can be just as majestic and memorable as any sun-kissed midday meal. Any time I can, I vote for building a blazing fire in the kitchen fireplace, ready for roasting guinea fowl on a spit, or to warm whole winter truffles, rubbed with truffle butter and wrapped in parchment, then foil, and set in the wood cinders just until the butter melts and permeates the cells of the magical mushroom. Holiday lunches in Provence are among the most memorable. I remember one Christmas when our friends Maggie and Al and their daughter Gigi joined us for a long holiday weekend. As we awoke on Christmas morning a light dusting of snow was already on the ground. It snowed wet, plump snowflakes all day long, until we were up to our ankles in the white surprise. We cooked a goose in the oven, opened oysters and champagne, and later went out into the vineyard with bright-red umbrellas and recorded the unexpected holiday with memorable photos we cherish to this day.

Whether it is a restaurant meal, one you prepare and share with friends, or one at which you are a guest at someone else's home, lunch in Provence always offers the potential of bringing you new levels of happiness, discovery, contentment. The possibilities are endless. Hope for a touch of serendipity, surprise, and renewal.

1.

Sharing good food and wine with someone you love is perfection.

Jean-André Charial

Paying attention to what you put in your body, eating leisurely, spending time at the table to converse with people you are close to— this is important.

Jean-André Charial

To begin with, I hate these new-fangled intermediate meals. Why can't people eat enough at luncheon to last till dinner?

Edith Wharton

Thinking, dreaming, and living food is the norm in Provence, where most people's days are geared around satisfying their passionate appetite for dining well. And not without good cause: Provençal cuisine is reputed the world over. Lazing over lunch with friends, leaving one vowing never to eat that much again (until tomorrow), is an integral part of the Provençal experience.

Nicola Williams, Catherine Le Nevez

And so with the sunshine and the great bursts of leaves growing on the trees, just as things grow in fast movies, I had that familiar conviction that life was beginning over again with the summer.

F. Scott Fitzgerald

Here in Provence people still sit down at a table for lunch. I have lunch every day with my wife—always—just one dish and a glass of wine, sometimes two. *Always the wine!*

Jean-André Charial

A quieter, more contemplative life, one punctuated only by the scraping of chairs after a leisurely lunch and the wind rustling through the lavender fields. . . .

Sara Clemence

Marseille soap or *Savon de Marseille* is a traditional soap that has been made in and around Marseille for around six hundred years by mixing seawater from the Mediterranean with vegetable oils. In 1688 Louis XIV introduced the Edict of Colbert that limited the use of the name *Savon de Marseille* to soaps made in the Marseille area, a law that still applies today.

I sing the love of a Provençal maid;
How through the wheat-fields of La Crau she strayed,
Following the fate that drew her to the sea.
Unbeknown beyond remote La Crau was she;
And I, who tell the rustic tale of her,
Would fain be Homer's humble follower.

Frédéric Mistral

... and then I have
nature and art and
poetry, and if that
is not enough,
what is enough?

If you truly love
nature, you will
find beauty
everywhere. . . .

Vincent van Gogh

In Paris today millions of pounds of bread are sold daily, made during the previous night by those strange, half-naked beings one glimpses through cellar windows, whose wild-seeming cries floating out of those depths always makes a painful impression. In the morning, one sees these pale men, still white with flour, carrying a loaf under one arm, going off to rest and gather new strength to renew their hard and useful labor when night comes again. I have always highly esteemed the brave and humble workers who labor all night to produce those soft but crusty loaves that look more like cake than bread.

Alexandre Dumas

The pizza-like dish **la pissaladière** is made in the regions of Nice, Marseille, Toulon, and Var. It is a type of white pizza, as no tomatoes are used, and is believed to have been introduced by the Avignon Papacy.

Make a classic bread dough and spread on to a baking tray. Top with a mixture of very slow-cooked onions and garlic, sautéed until they are creamy, Niçoise olives, and anchovies or sardines. Serve hot or cold as an appetizer or as a tasty main course accompanied by a salad. Also makes a perfect picnic dish.

Pain d'epi (below, right) is a classic French bread that is shaped to resemble a wheat stalk. **Fougasse** is the traditional bread of Provence and is round and flat with holes cut out by the baker. Modern versions are baked with olives or nuts inside.

There are
few things so
pleasant as a picnic
lunch eaten in
perfect comfort.

William Somerset Maugham

2.

The better the ingredients you use, the better your meal will be.

Jean-André Charial

Provence: that felicitous corner of France where vegetables taste great, herbs are potent, garlic abundant, and olive oil indispensable in cooking.

Hrayr Berberoglu

Sunflowers, circa 1888
Vincent van Gogh (1853–1890)
Van Gogh's fame comes largely from his work in Provence, although he lived there for just a few years, from 1888 until his death.

Cooking is an art and patience a virtue.... Careful shopping, fresh ingredients, and an unhurried approach are nearly all you need. There is one more thing—love. Love for food and love for those you invite to your table. With a combination of these things you can be an artist—not perhaps in the representational style of a Dutch master, but rather more like Gauguin, the naïve, or Van Gogh, the impressionist. Plates or pictures of sunshine taste of happiness and love.

Keith Floyd

Provence is one of the great garden destinations of the world. It is a special place where the beauty of its natural landscape has magically mingled with civilizations for centuries and the beauty keeps on radiating.

Bonnie Manion

My philosophy is to always use the best products, and the best way to obtain the best products is to produce them yourself.

—

I like the idea that when the roots develop and go down into the soil, their bounty provides an expression of this part of the earth.

Jean-André Charial

Pistou is the Provençal equivalent of Italian pesto, usually made with fresh basil ground and mixed with olive oil, along with summer vegetables, such as white beans, green beans, tomatoes, summer squash, and potatoes, and served either hot or cold. It is also the basis for *soupe au pistou*, Provence's version of minestrone.

Herbes de Provence (Provençal herbs) are an assortment of herbs commonly used in Provençal cooking containing a combination of thyme, sage, rosemary, basil, lavender, savory, fennel seed, marjoram, tarragon, oregano, and bay leaf.
A **bouquet garni** combines thyme, bay leaf, parsley, leek, and celery. Fresh herbs are tied together with string, dried herbs are bundled into a cheesecloth pouch.

PROVENÇAL VEGETABLES WITH PESTO

Tous les légumes de Provence au pistou

SERVES 4

½ cup (70 g) shelled peas

⅓ cup (50 g) green beans, de-stalked

¼ cup (40 g) fresh *haricot coco* beans

1 sprig of fresh thyme

1 small sprig of fresh rosemary

pinch of salt

1 generous tablespoon (20 g) butter

2 teaspoons olive oil

1 medium-sized onion (60 g), peeled and finely diced

2 stalks of celery (40 g), finely diced

1 carrot (60 g), peeled and finely diced

1 turnip root (60 g), peeled and finely diced

⅔ cup (100 g) fresh outdoor tomatoes, skinned, deseeded, and quartered

1 firm-fleshed potato (40 g), peeled and finely diced

5 cloves garlic, unpeeled and crushed

6⅓ cups (1.5 liters) chicken stock

1 zucchini (40 g), finely diced

generous ½ cup (100 g) shaved Parmesan

freshly ground black pepper to taste

For the pesto

5 cloves of garlic, peeled

1 bunch of fresh green basil leaves

⅔ cup (150 ml) extra-virgin olive oil

pinch of fleur de sel (or coarse sea salt)

Blanch the peas and green beans together, then thinly slice the beans.

Place the haricot beans in a small saucepan, add cold water and bring to a boil. Add the thyme and rosemary and simmer lightly. Add a pinch of salt.

In a casserole, melt the butter with a teaspoon of olive oil. Add the garlic and all the vegetables except the zucchini. Cook for a minute. Add the chicken stock, bring to a boil, then add the diced zucchini.

Pesto

Put the garlic cloves in a mortar with a pinch of salt and grind with the pestle. Add the basil leaves and continue to grind until you have a smooth paste. Add the olive oil and season to taste.

To serve

Serve the vegetables and pesto in individual bowls, topped with Parmesan, a teaspoon of olive oil, and freshly ground black pepper.

RED MULLET WITH SPRING VEGETABLES, PESTO, CROUTONS, AND TAPENADE

Filet de rouget avec artichauts et jeunes légumes de saison, pistou de basilic et croûtons dorés à la tapenade noire

SERVES 6

$\frac{3}{4}$ cup (200 g) cauliflower, divided into florets

3 cups (750 ml) chicken stock

pinch of saffron

1 bunch of spring onions (150 g), cleaned and chopped

1 tablespoon (15 ml) olive oil

2 artichokes, trimmed

juice of half a lemon

salt and freshly ground black pepper to taste

1 sprig of fresh thyme

1 clove of garlic, peeled and halved

1 cup (300 g) each of chopped fresh seasonal vegetables—zucchini, asparagus, peas, broad beans (podded)

1 tablespoon (15 g) butter

6 sundried tomatoes, roughly chopped

$\frac{1}{4}$ cup (60 g) black olives, pitted (preferably Taggiascan, a small, fruity Italian olive, but any black olives will do)

handful of chives, chopped

12 pieces of red mullet (about 4 oz./120 g each)

6 croutons

$\frac{1}{3}$ cup (60 g) black olive tapenade

For the basil pesto

1 bunch of basil

$\frac{2}{3}$ cup (150 ml) olive oil

2 cloves of garlic, peeled

Make the pesto by blanching the basil leaves, then refreshing in iced water. Blend the basil together with the oil and garlic to make a smooth green oil.

Cook the cauliflower in the chicken stock with the saffron until al dente. Drain, and keep the stock.

In a saucepan, sweat the onion in the olive oil, then add the artichokes, lemon juice, salt, pepper, thyme, and garlic. Fill the pan halfway with water, cover, and cook until the artichokes are al dente. Keep them in their cooking water.

In a large quantity of salted boiling water cook the other vegetables. When cooked, refresh in chilled water. Put all the vegetables together in a large pan with the stock from the cauliflower and the butter. Heat them through then add the sundried tomatoes, olives, chives, and pesto.

Cook the fish fillets in a little olive oil in a non-stick pan until crisp.

To serve

Top each crouton with a teaspoon of tapenade. Place the vegetables on plates and top with the fish and croutons.

When produce is so fresh you can eat it raw, right then and there; treat it with respect and it will respect you back.

—

Vegetables show you the way to follow the seasons: peas in March and April, asparagus in April, string beans in June and July, tomatoes in August, and so on.

Jean-André Charial

RED MULLET WITH GRAPEFRUIT

Marinière de rouget au pamplemousse

SERVES 6

12 fillets of red mullet (about 4 oz./120 g each)

For the fish

$4\frac{1}{4}$ cups (1 liter) chicken stock

1 clove garlic, peeled and crushed

1 tomato, peeled and chopped

6 threads of saffron

2 grapefruit

For the vegetables

$2\frac{1}{2}$ cups (500 g) of fresh seasonal vegetables of your choice— sliced green beans, thinly sliced carrots, peas, podded broad beans, thinly sliced shallots

scant $\frac{1}{2}$ cup (100 ml) olive oil

2 tablespoons rice vinegar

juice of 1 grapefruit

1 teaspoon soy sauce

1 teaspoon honey

3 basil leaves, chopped

salt and freshly ground black pepper to taste

8 yellow cherry tomatoes

8 red cherry tomatoes

1 red bell pepper, diced

1 green bell pepper, diced

1 yellow bell pepper, diced

fresh flat-leaved parsley to garnish

Fish

Bring the chicken stock to a boil. Add the garlic, tomato, saffron, juice and zest of two of the grapefruit (reserve several slices to use as garnish). Let the mixture infuse for 30 minutes. Strain, then lightly poach the fish in this stock. Reserve the stock.

Vegetables

In a large quantity of salted boiling water, cook the seasonal vegetables until al dente. Prepare the vinaigrette by mixing together the olive oil, vinegar, grapefruit juice, soy sauce, honey, basil, salt, and pepper. Toss the hot vegetables, and cherry tomatoes, in the vinaigrette.

To serve

Place the fillets of fish in the center of a plate, then surround with vegetables. Pour over the hot stock and scatter the diced bell peppers on top. Just before serving, sprinkle with chopped parsley and garnish with slices of peeled grapefruit.

Courgette is the French word for zucchini. Along with tomatoes and eggplants, it is a key ingredient in ratatouille.

STUFFED ZUCCHINI FLOWERS

Fleurs de courgettes farcies

SERVES 4

16 zucchini, with flowers attached

salt and freshly ground black pepper to taste

For the batter

1 cup (100 g) flour

1⅖ oz. (40 g) baker's yeast

generous 1⅓ cups (330 ml) beer

approximately 1 cup (250 ml) peanut oil

For the stuffing

½ cup (50 g) eggplant, finely chopped

⅔ cup (150 ml) olive oil

scant ½ cup (50 g) toasted breadcrumbs

20 pine nuts, toasted

2 tablespoons (20 g) shaved Parmesan

½ clove garlic, chopped

4 tablespoons (10 g) fresh flat-leaved parsley

1 tablespoon (10 g) pitted black olives

For the vinaigrette

scant ½ cup (100 ml) olive oil

2 tablespoons (30 ml) balsamic vinegar

Battered zucchini flowers (prepare the day before)

Remove the flowers from four zucchini, rinse, and set the zucchini aside. Make an incision in the base of each flower and remove the stamen.

Sieve the flour and baker's yeast into a bowl and pour in the beer, whisking quickly to avoid lumps. Leave to rest for 1 hour.

Heat the peanut oil in a small pan—the oil should be about ½ in. (1 cm) deep. Don't let it get too hot; avoid making the oil sputter. Brush the batter on to the open sides of the flowers. Fry the battered side of each flower in the peanut oil until lightly golden, being careful not to let it brown.

Place on an oven tray in a 140°F (60°C) oven and bake for 2 hours. Leaving the door closed, turn off the oven and leave the flowers overnight to dry out completely.

Stuffed zucchini

Preheat the oven to 390°F (200°C).

Finely chop the four zucchini that you set aside the day before. Sauté the zucchini and eggplant in the olive oil until lightly browned. Drain on a paper towel.

Bring a large pot of water to a boil. Cook the remaining zucchini in the water for 3 minutes, making sure that the flowers are out of the water but remain attached. Then immerse the flowers in the boiling water for 1 minute.

Blend the sautéed eggplant and zucchini, breadcrumbs, pine nuts, Parmesan, garlic, parsley, and olives into a paste, then season with salt and pepper. Stuff each of the twelve zucchini flowers until three-quarters full. Close the flowers, then place the zucchini on a baking dish, and cook for 10–12 minutes.

To serve

Make a vinaigrette with the olive oil, balsamic vinegar, salt, and pepper.

Place the baked zucchini on plates and sprinkle with vinaigrette. Garnish each plate with a battered zucchini flower.

Tell me what you eat: I will tell you what you are.

Jean Anthelme Brillat-Savarin

The secret of a good ratatouille is to cook the vegetables separately so each will taste truly of itself.

Joël Robuchon

Ratatouille is a traditional Provençal stewed vegetable dish usually served as a side dish, but can also be served as a meal on its own accompanied by pasta, rice, or bread.

There is much debate on how to make a traditional ratatouille. One method is to simply sauté all of the vegetables together. Some cooks, including Julia Child, insist on a layering approach, where the eggplant and the zucchini are sautéed separately, while the tomatoes, onion, garlic, and bell peppers are made into a sauce. The ratatouille is then layered in a casserole—eggplant, zucchini, tomato and bell pepper mixture—then baked in an oven. A third method, favored by chef Joël Robuchon, is similar except that the ingredients are recombined in a large pot and simmered instead of baked in an oven.

Slice one red and one green bell pepper that have been roasted with skins and seeds removed into $\frac{2}{5}$-inch (1-centimeter) strips, and sauté. Blanch four tomatoes, remove skins and seeds, and roughly chop. Chop one onion, three small zucchini, and one medium-sized eggplant and sauté each separately in olive oil until each vegetable browns. Combine all the ingredients in a heavy-bottomed pan or Dutch oven; add five cloves of chopped garlic, a dash or two of olive oil, and salt and pepper. Cover and cook over a low to medium heat for 30 minutes or until very tender. Add chopped herbes de Provence (basil, thyme, oregano, marjoram, or other herbs of your preference) and season to taste.

3 onions, peeled and sliced

4 cloves of garlic, peeled and chopped

5 tablespoons olive oil

2 lb. (1 kg) eggplant, peeled and chopped

2 lb. (1 kg) zucchini, peeled and chopped

2 green bell peppers, deseeded and chopped

2 red bell peppers, deseeded and chopped

2 lb. (1 kg) tomatoes, peeled, deseeded, and cut into large chunks

salt and freshly ground black pepper to taste

grated Parmesan to garnish

RATATOUILLE NIÇOISE

Cook the onions and garlic in 2 tablespoons of the olive oil until lightly browned.

Add the eggplant, zucchini and bell peppers; cook for a few minutes, then add the tomatoes.

Add the remaining olive oil and simmer over a low heat until vegetables are tender.

Season with salt and pepper. Sprinkle with Parmesan.

Delicious hot or cold.

4 portions sea bass
(about 4 oz./120 g each)

1 tablespoon (15 ml) olive oil

1 clove garlic

1 sprig of fresh thyme

juice of 1 lemon

For the ratatouille

1 each small red and yellow bell pepper
(prepared as below)

1 tablespoon (15 ml) olive oil

1 eggplant, diced

3 small zucchini, diced

12 cloves of garlic, unpeeled and crushed

1 bouquet garni

fleur de sel (or coarse sea salt) to taste

freshly ground black pepper to taste

pinch of *piment d'Espelette* pepper
(or mild chilli pepper)

3 Roma plum tomatoes, peeled,
deseeded, and chopped

3 tablespoons (30 g) pitted green olives
(preferably Maussane, a Provençal olive,
but any green olives will do), diced

GRILLED SEA BASS WITH RATATOUILLE

Dos de loup de méditerranée cuit à la plancha, fine ratatouille aux goûts d'ici

Bake the bell peppers in a 410°F (210°C) oven for 30 minutes. Remove from oven, then seal in a plastic bag for 15 minutes. Strain, and save the juice for later. Discard the stems, seeds, and white flesh. Dice.

Add oil to a skillet, cook the eggplant until al dente. Do the same with the zucchini. Drain.

Place the garlic, eggplant, zucchini, and bouquet garni in a casserole. Season with the salt, pepper, and *piment d'Espelette* pepper, then add the tomatoes, bell peppers, bell pepper juice, and olives and stew for a few minutes.

Grill the fish in the olive oil in a frying pan seasoned with garlic and thyme until brown. When cooked, season with lemon juice.

Serve with the ratatouille.

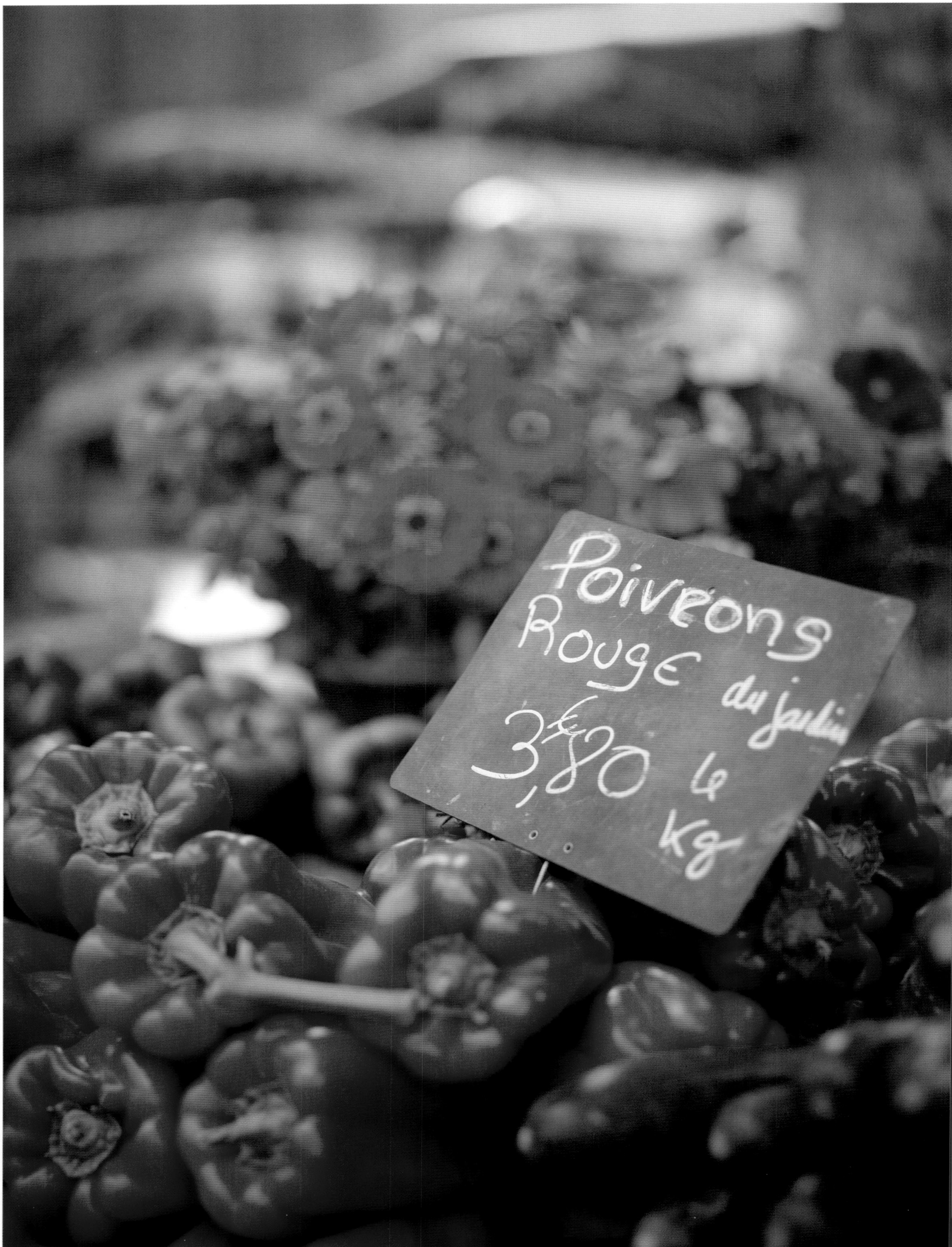
Poivrons
Rouge du jardi
3,80 € le
kg

Rouille is a mayonnaise with red pimentos that is often spread on to bread and added to fish soups, in particular the traditional *bouillabaisse* served in Marseille.

16 poivrade artichokes (small purple artichokes from Provence)

juice of 2 lemons

$3\frac{1}{2}$ oz. (100 g) smoked bacon, cut into chunks

scant $\frac{1}{2}$ cup (100 ml) olive oil

2 carrots, peeled and diced

1 large onion, peeled and finely chopped

$3\frac{1}{3}$ cups (200 g) girolles or golden chanterelle mushrooms, de-stalked, trimmed, and quartered

salt and freshly ground black pepper to taste

1 bay leaf

several sprigs of fresh thyme, chopped

8 large cloves of garlic, peeled

$\frac{2}{3}$ cup (150 ml) white wine

water to cover

fresh flat-leaved parsley and extra thyme, chopped, to garnish

ARTICHOKE BARIGOULE

Artichauts barigoule

Preheat oven to 340°F (170°C). Trim the artichokes, removing the tough outer leaves. Cut into quarters and soak in water with the lemon juice while you prepare the bacon.

Blanch the bacon for 1 minute in boiling water.

Drain the artichokes and dry them. Heat the olive oil in a casserole and cook the artichokes over a high heat for 3 minutes.

Add the carrots, cook for a further 2 minutes then add the onion and the bacon, cooking for 2 more minutes.

Add the mushrooms, cook for 2 more minutes. Season with salt and pepper, then add the bay leaf, thyme, and garlic.

Add the white wine, then enough water to completely cover the vegetables. Cover and bake for 15 minutes.

Take the casserole out of the oven and place it on a hot stove top. Remove the lid and boil rapidly to reduce the cooking juice. Adjust seasoning to suit.

Sprinkle the parsley and thyme over the artichokes. Cover for 30–60 seconds to bring out the flavor.

Serve in the casserole dish.

24 poivrade artichokes, trimmed (small purple artichokes from Provence)

juice of 1 lemon

2 cups (500 ml) olive oil

$3\frac{1}{2}$ oz. (100 g) smoked pork belly, coarsely chopped

2 white onions, peeled and thinly sliced

3 carrots, peeled and thinly sliced

4 cloves of garlic, crushed

salt and freshly ground black pepper to taste

$1\frac{2}{3}$ cups (400 ml) dry white wine

$1\frac{1}{4}$ cups (1 liter) chicken stock

1 tablespoon (15 g) butter

$\frac{1}{2}$ cup (100 g) crushed green olives

$5\frac{1}{3}$ oz. (150 g) dry chorizo, cut into thin slices

1 tablespoon (15 ml) olive oil

pinch of fleur de sel (or coarse sea salt)

For the bouquet garnis and herb pouches

green leaves of 2 leeks

1 sprig of fresh parsley

2 sprigs of fresh thyme

1 stalk of celery, cut in two

$\frac{3}{4}$ teaspoon black peppercorns

1 teaspoon coriander seeds

cheesecloth and string

PURPLE ARTICHOKES WITH CHORIZO AND CRUSHED OLIVES

Artichauts violets en barigoule, avec chorizo et olives cassées de la vallée des Baux de Provence

Prepare two bouquet garnis and two little cheesecloth pouches each of peppercorns and coriander seeds; see page 65.

Soak the artichokes in cold water and the lemon juice while you prepare the pork.

Heat the olive oil in a casserole. Lightly brown the pork belly then add the drained artichokes, vegetables, garlic, bouquets garnis, and pouches. Add salt and sweat the mixture for 3 minutes. Deglaze with the white wine, cook until reduced by three-quarters, then add the chicken stock. Simmer partially covered for 6 minutes, then remove the artichokes.

Add the butter to the pan juices and reduce by half. Strain the juice and add the olives to it. Adjust the seasoning.

Arrange the chorizo, artichokes, juice, and olives on a plate. Drizzle with olive oil and freshly ground pepper. Add a few grains of fleur de sel and serve.

This dish can be served hot or cold depending on the season.

If I can't have too
many truffles, I'll
do without truffles.

Sidonie-Gabrielle Colette

Her whole being
dilated in an
atmosphere of
luxury; it was the
background she
required, the only
climate she could
breathe in.

Edith Wharton

ASPARAGUS WITH SLOW-COOKED EGGS, MUSHROOMS, AND TRUFFLES

L'asperge du gard braisée au jus de volaille et aux morilles, oeuf de poule cuit à basse température et truffe d'été 'tuber aestivum'

SERVES 6

6 free-range eggs, shells cleaned with a soft brush

3 shallots (100 g), peeled and chopped

3 cups (200 g) morel mushrooms, peeled and halved

2½ lb. (1.2 kg) green asparagus, washed and peeled, cut in halves diagonally

pinch of salt

3½ tablespoons (50 g) butter

2 cups (500 ml) chicken stock

dash of sherry vinegar

salt and freshly ground pepper to taste

3 oz. (80 g) summer truffles, shaved

For the jus de volaille

2 lb. (1 kg) chicken carcass

4¼ cups (1 liter) chicken stock

Eggs

Cook the eggs in a steam oven at 155°F (68°C) for about 30 minutes. After cooking refresh in iced water.

At least 15 minutes before serving, put the eggs in hot water (140°F/60°C).

Jus de volaille

Caramelize the chicken. Cover with the chicken stock, then cook for at least 30 minutes over a gentle heat. Strain. You should have a brown-colored, non-reduced *jus de volaille*.

Vegetables

In a pan sauté the shallots until cooked but not brown. Add the mushrooms and sauté for 2 minutes over a very low heat, then add the asparagus, a pinch of salt, and the butter, tossing all together to make sure the vegetables are coated. Deglaze with the chicken stock. Fill the pan halfway with the *jus de volaille*. Cover and cook for 2 minutes. Remove the lid and cook until the juice has properly blended. Season with a dash of sherry vinegar, salt, and pepper.

To serve

Remove the shell from each egg and place the egg in the center of a serving dish. Add salt and freshly ground black pepper, the asparagus, and the mushrooms, then the cooking juice. Finish with a few truffle shavings.

Serve with thin slices of bread and shaved truffles.

Getting the best is what inspires me. Good food is always about quality.

—

The best food is the simplest—it should just be an expression of the produce and then it is *très bon*.

Jean-André Charial

3.

A cook constantly draws inspiration from the local surroundings.

Jean-André Charial

Art is a harmony parallel with nature.

Paul Cézanne

In the nineteenth and twentieth centuries, many well-known painters in the world converged on Provence. They were drawn by the clarity of the light. This clarity is caused, in part, by the mistral wind that increases visibility by removing dust from the atmosphere.

Route de la Gineste, near Marseille, 1859
Paul Camille Guigou (1834–1871)
Guigou was an impressionist painter who studied in Marseille and painted mostly Provençal landscapes. His nine-year painting career was cut short by his early death, and his work went virtually unnoticed in his lifetime.

The quality of the light in Provence is unique and it influences your cooking— the heat, the produce, the environment.

Jean-André Charial

The Mediterranean village of **Menton**, nicknamed the Pearl of France,
has a warm microclimate favorable to tangerine, orange, and lemon groves,
hence one of the town's symbols, the lemon.

Huge lemons, cut in slices, would sink like setting suns into the dusky sea, softly illuminating it with their radiating membranes, and its clear, smooth surface aquiver from the rising bitter essence.

Rainer Maria Rilke

Poster by **Hugo d'Alesi**
for Menton, City of Lemons,
circa 1900

16 green asparagus, peeled	5 egg yolks
16 white asparagus, peeled	$5\frac{1}{3}$ oz. (150 g) clarified butter
3 cups (200 g) fresh morel mushrooms	juice of 1 lemon
2 shallots, peeled and chopped	fleur de sel (or coarse sea salt) to taste
$3\frac{1}{2}$ tablespoons (50 g) butter	freshly ground black pepper to taste
generous $\frac{3}{4}$ cup (200 ml) Vin Jaune d'Arbois (or dry white wine or dry sherry)	fresh herbs to garnish
scant $\frac{1}{2}$ cup (100 ml) chicken stock	

GREEN AND WHITE ASPARAGUS WITH MORELS

Asperges vertes et blanches, morilles sauce mousseline

Asparagus

Peel the asparagus, then tie in bundles of eight. Cook in heavily salted boiling water for 6 minutes. When cooked, untie the bundles and trim the ends diagonally.

Morels

Rinse the morels in warm water. Sweat the shallots in the butter, add the morels, then deglaze with half the wine. Cook until reduced by half, then add the chicken stock. Simmer for about 10 minutes then remove from the heat.

Mousseline sauce

In a pan, but not over heat, emulsify the egg yolks along with the rest of the wine.

Cook over a moderate heat, whisking as it cooks, to obtain a light and frothy sauce. Cool slightly, then gradually add the clarified butter. Add the lemon juice just before serving.

To serve

Spread the mousseline sauce on the base of a serving plate, then arrange the asparagus and morels on top. Season with salt and pepper, and dress with herbs of your choice.

LEMON TARTS

Tartelette gourmande au citron confit

SERVES 6

For the lemon cream

scant ½ cup (3 oz./90 g) granulated sugar

1 stick (4 oz./110 g) butter

¼ cup (60 ml) lemon juice

1 egg

1 egg yolk

For the sweet pastry shells

generous ½ cup (2 ½ oz./75 g) confectioners' sugar

1 ¾ cups (6 oz./175 g) flour

pinch of salt

7 tablespoons (3 ½ oz./100 g) butter

1 egg

For the meringue

scant ½ cup (3 ½ oz./100 g) egg whites (about 4 egg whites)

¼ cup (1 ¾ oz./50 g) confectioners' sugar

¼ cup (1 ¾ oz./50 g) finely granulated sugar

zest of 1 lime

For the lemon sorbet

scant ½ cup (100 ml) water

½ cup (3 ½ oz./100 g) granulated sugar

scant ½ cup (100 ml) lemon juice

scant ½ cup (100 ml) milk

Lemon cream

Bring the ingredients to a boil, whisking vigorously. Cool and set aside.

Sweet pastry

Mix together the confectioners' sugar, flour and salt. Add the butter and gently rub it in. Add the egg, mixing it thoroughly into the mixture. Cover in plastic wrap and refrigerate for 20 minutes.

Preheat the oven to 410°F (210°C). Roll out the resulting pastry dough and fit into tart molds. Cover with baking paper and pie-weights or dry lentils (to prevent the pastry from rising). Cook for 25 minutes. Cool and remove the paper and lentils.

Meringue

Lower the oven temperature to 210°F (100°C). Beat the egg whites, then gently add the confectioners' sugar and finely granulated sugar. When the mixture is stiff, add the lime zest. Spoon in little balls on to an oven tray and bake for 2 hours. Cool.

Lemon sorbet

Bring the water and sugar to a boil. Cool, then add the lemon juice then the milk. Process in an ice-cream maker.

To serve

Fill the sweet pastry tarts with the lemon cream and top with the meringues. Serve with the sorbet.

Côte d'Azur, 1889
Paul Signac (1863–1935)
Signac visited Saint-Tropez in 1892, and bought a villa, La Hune, at the foot of a citadel in 1897. It was at his villa that his friend Henri Matisse painted his famous *Luxe, Calme et Volupté* in 1904. Signac made numerous paintings along the coast.

Blue Nude IV, 1952
Henri Matisse (1869–1954)
Matisse moved to Nice in 1917, where he became enamored of the silver clarity of light.

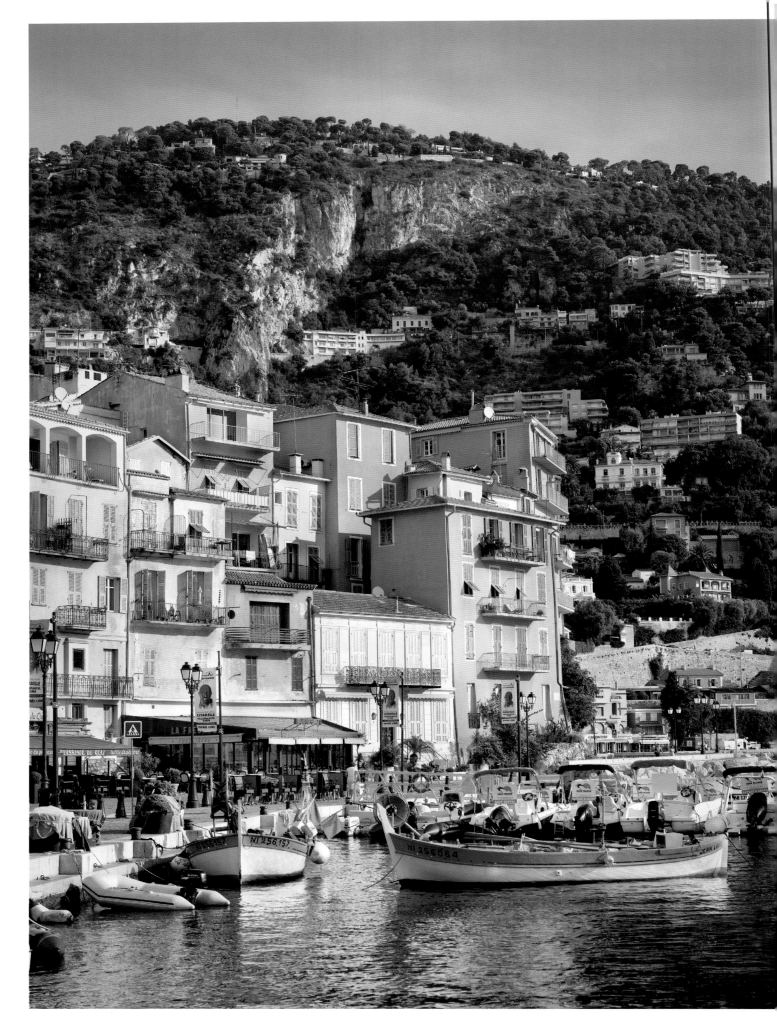

Fish in the hands of a skilled cook can become an inexhaustible source of gustatory pleasures.

Jean Anthelme Brillat-Savarin

Two fish are most often found on menus in Provence: the **rouget** (red mullet) and the **loup** (sea bass). Both are usually grilled, the latter over grapevine wood.

SEA BASS ON ROASTED RISOTTO CAKES WITH CALAMARI, FENNEL, CHORIZO, ZUCCHINI, AND SLOW-ROASTED TOMATO SAUCE

Dos de loup cuit lentement sur sa peau croustillante, risotto rôti au sirop de tomate épicée, fenouil et encornet juste saisis à la plancha et chorizo

SERVES 6

For the risotto cakes

1 small onion (50 g), peeled and finely chopped

generous ¾ cup (200 ml) olive oil

2 cups (400 g) risotto rice (Carnaroli is best)

4¼ cups (1 liter) chicken stock, heated

generous ½ cup (100 g) grated Parmesan

2 tablespoons flour

1 tablespoon (15 ml) olive oil

For the slow-roasted tomato sauce

1 small onion (50 g), peeled and chopped

2 cloves of garlic, peeled and chopped

1 tablespoon (15 ml) olive oil

⅓ cup (20 g) celery, chopped

⅓ cup (20 g) fresh ginger, peeled and finely chopped

1 lb. (500 g) fresh tomatoes, peeled, deseeded, and cut into quarters

1 cup (250 ml) tomato juice, or tomato purée

salt and freshly ground black pepper to taste

1 tablespoon granulated sugar

Tabasco sauce to taste

For the fish

6 fillets of sea bass (about 4 oz./120 g each)

2 tablespoons (30 ml) olive oil

7 oz. (200 g) of fresh calamari, cleaned and thinly sliced

1½ oz. (40 g) chorizo, cut into julienne strips

2 small zucchini (300 g), cut into julienne strips

2 cups (400 g) fennel, finely chopped

handful of mixed fresh herbs (tarragon, chervil, dill)

4 tablespoons (40 g) olives, halved and pitted (preferably Taggiascan, a small, fruity Italian olive, but any black olives will do)

reduced balsamic vinegar to garnish (optional)

Risotto cakes

Sweat the onion in olive oil. Add the rice, stir, and let it cook until it becomes pearly colored. Add the warmed stock, about a cup at a time, stirring continuously. When the rice is cooked but still firm to the bite, remove from the heat, stir in the Parmesan, and spread the risotto on to a plate in a layer about ½ in. (1 cm) thick. Cool in the refrigerator.

Once cool, cut the risotto cake into approximately 3 in. (8 cm) squares. Flour the squares, place in a baking dish, and sprinkle with olive oil, then roast in the oven until lightly browned. Set aside until you're ready to serve.

Slow-roasted tomato sauce

Sweat the onion and garlic in an ovenproof pan with enough olive oil to coat, then add the celery, ginger, and tomatoes. Add the tomato juice or purée. Season lightly with salt and pepper, and add about a tablespoon of sugar. Season with Tabasco to taste. Place baking paper on top to prevent evaporation, then bake at 360°F (180°C) for an hour. Remove from the oven and add further seasoning to taste.

Fish

Season the fish fillets on both sides and place them skin-side down in a non-stick pan with a tablespoon of olive oil. Briefly cook both sides— about 3 minutes for the skin side and 2 minutes for the other side.

In a heated pan (with no oil), layer the calamari, chorizo, zucchini, and fennel, dividing each layer with the herbs and halved olives in between. Without stirring, continue to heat, then quickly add a tablespoon of olive oil and season.

To serve

Place a risotto cake on each plate and carefully turn out a serving of the layered calamari, chorizo, zucchini, and fennel on to each cake. Place the fish on top and garnish with a reduced balsamic glaze (optional) on the plate. Serve with the tomato sauce on the side or in a small jug.

$4\frac{1}{2}$ lb. (2 kg) mussels

2 glasses white wine

1 shallot, chopped

scant $\frac{1}{2}$ cup (100 ml) whipping cream, 30 percent fat content

pinch of powdered saffron

2 tablespoons (30 g) butter

1 tablespoon breadcrumbs

MUSSEL GRATIN

Moules gratinées

Preheat the oven to 360°F (180°C).

Put the mussels in a large saucepan with the wine and shallot. Cook until the mussels are open, then drain them, keeping the liquid. Remove half of the shells from the mussels, and place shell-side down in a gratin dish.

Strain the liquid then put it back in the saucepan with the cream and saffron. Cook rapidly until the liquid is reduced by half.

Add the butter, pour the sauce over the mussels, sprinkle with the breadcrumbs, and bake in the oven for about 5 minutes.

Cod is commonly found on French menus and the ways of cooking it are many and varied. *Brandade de morue* is traditionally a thick creamy purée made of salted cod crushed and mixed with olive oil, milk, garlic, and sometimes truffles. A quick and easy version is to simply mix salted cod with aioli, a garlic mayonnaise.

French red rascasse, or scorpionfish, is abundant in the Mediterranean and an essential ingredient in bouillabaisse but can also be cooked on its own.

Bouillabaisse is the classic seafood dish of Marseille. The traditional version is made with three fish: scorpionfish, sea robin, and European conger, as well as an assortment of other fish and shellfish such as John Dory, monkfish, sea urchins, crabs, and sea spiders. The seasoning is as important as the fish, including salt, pepper, onion, tomato, saffron, fennel, sage, thyme, bay leaf, sometimes orange peel, and a cup of white wine or cognac. In Marseille the fish and the broth are served separately, with the broth served over thick slices of bread with rouille.

Bourride is similar to bouillabaisse except that it does not contain tomato and is thickened with aioli, another traditional Provençal concoction.

Escabeche is a popular seafood dish where the fish, usually sardines, is marinated overnight in vinegar or citrus juice, then is either poached or fried.

BOUILLABAISSE

SERVES 6

For the broth

2 lb. (1 kg) rockfish, unscaled and gutted

$\frac{1}{4}$ cup (60 ml) olive oil

1 bulb of garlic cloves, peeled and crushed

6 sprigs of fresh parsley, chopped

2 leeks, rinsed and thickly sliced

2 onions, peeled and finely chopped

6 fresh fennel stalks, chopped

4 tomatoes, crushed

2 bay leaves

zest of 1 orange

1 chilli pepper, chopped

$12\frac{2}{3}$ cups (3 liters) boiling water

2 pinches of powdered saffron

salt and freshly ground black pepper to taste

For the fish

6 potatoes, peeled and cut into large pieces

20 slices bread

1 clove of garlic, peeled

4 scorpionfish, scaled and gutted

4 vives (weeverfish), scaled and gutted

4 slices conger eel

1 whole John Dory or Saint Pierre (about 2 lb./1 kg), scaled and gutted

salt and freshly ground black pepper to taste

aioli to accompany
(see recipe on page 161)

Broth

Rinse the rockfish.

In a saucepan, over a low heat, sauté the garlic, parsley, and vegetables with the olive oil, bay leaves, orange peel and chilli pepper. Brown for 15 minutes. Add the rockfish and season. Let this cook for 15 minutes then add the boiling water. Simmer for another 10 minutes. Remove from the heat, then take out the fennel and the orange peel.

Strain the vegetables through a Mouli grater or sieve and discard the vegetables. You should have about 10 cups of fish broth.

Add the saffron to the broth, and season if required.

Fish

Boil the potatoes in equal amounts of the fish broth and water in a cast-iron pan for about 30 minutes. Season and put the potatoes aside.

Toast the slices of bread, then rub with the garlic. Cut into croutons, place in a tureen.

Bring the remaining fish broth to a boil. Starting with the firmer flesh, poach the fish over a low heat for 6–10 minutes.

To serve

Arrange the potatoes on a large platter then lay the fish on the potatoes.

Pour the broth into the tureen, on top of the croutons.

Serve accompanied by aioli.

2 scorpionfish, gutted and cleaned, with spines removed

scant $\frac{1}{2}$ cup (100 ml) white wine

salt and freshly ground black pepper to taste

For the stuffing

scant $\frac{1}{2}$ cup (100 ml) milk

$1\frac{1}{2}$ cups (100 g) crustless white bread, broken into pieces

$5\frac{1}{2}$ tablespoons (80 g) butter

4 cups (250 g) button mushrooms, finely chopped

2 onions, peeled and finely chopped

1 shallot, peeled and finely chopped

2 cloves of garlic, peeled and finely chopped

1 cup (150 g) green chard, rinsed, delicately spun dry and chopped

salt and freshly ground black pepper to taste

1 egg

1 bunch of fresh parsley, rinsed, finely chopped then spun dry

SCORPIONFISH WITH VEGETABLE STUFFING

Rascasse farcie aux petits légumes

Stuffing

Heat the milk, then pour over the bread. Let soften, then crush with a fork.

Heat $3\frac{1}{2}$ tablespoons (50 g) of the butter in a saucepan. Add the mushrooms, onions, shallot, and garlic. Soften them, then add the chopped chard. Stir, then season with salt and pepper.

In a bowl combine the steamed chard and vegetable mixture with the bread, egg, and chopped parsley. Season, and mix with a fork.

Fish

Pat dry the fish with paper towels then stuff with the prepared stuffing.

Place the stuffed fish in a buttered baking dish. Drizzle with white wine and scatter with knobs of the remaining butter. Bake in a 410°F (210°C) oven for 20 minutes. Let stand, then serve hot.

131

Some spots are the cradle of genius. Provence is one.

Lawrence Durrell

4.

Great chefs express their feelings through their food.

Jean-André Charial

When you drink my wine
I want you to be able to feel the
heat of Provence, and see the
olive trees all around you.

Jean-André Charial

In Provence, olive oil is king.

Mark R. Vogel

The whole Mediterranean—the sculptures, the palms, the gold beads, the bearded heroes, the wine, the ideas, the ships, the moonlight, the winged gorgons, the bronze men, the philosophers—all of it seems to rise in the sour, pungent taste of these black olives between the teeth. A taste older than meat, older than wine. A taste as old as cold water.

Lawrence Durrell

Olives Grecques
Colossal
12€,80 Kilo

The **Cailletier** is a type of olive grown near Nice. It is also known as the Niçoise olive, after the way it is cured in the Nice area. It is a key ingredient in the Niçoise salad and can be used to make olive oil.

Niçoise salad, or Salade Niçoise, is a specialty of Nice for which it is named. A bed of lettuce is arranged on a flat plate and topped with ripe tomato wedges, halved boiled new potatoes, steamed green beans, wedges of hard-boiled eggs, tuna, and Niçoise olives, and, finally, garnished with tinned anchovies and served with a vinaigrette.

Traditional French recipes often clearly state that no cooked vegetables are to be used. Some say that it was Julia Child who first brought the Niçoise salad to the United States.

The classical Provençal way is a first course accompanied by a salad (the vinaigrette stimulates the appetite), then fish, followed by meat, vegetables, cheese, and dessert. Light to heavy. It makes for easier digestion.

Jean-André Charial

$2\frac{1}{2}$ cups (400 g) tomatoes, sliced

salt and freshly ground black pepper to taste

4 oz. (120 g) mozzarella, sliced

1 tablespoon balsamic vinegar

4 tablespoons olive oil

pinch of salt

fresh basil and seasonal herbs to garnish

TOMATOES AND MOZZARELLA

Tomates mozzarella

Arrange the tomato slices around the edge of a plate, each piece overlapping the previous one. Season with salt and pepper. Place the mozzarella slices on the tomatoes.

Make a vinaigrette with the balsamic vinegar, olive oil, and a pinch of salt. Drizzle the vinaigrette over the tomatoes and mozzarella.

Just before eating, garnish with the basil and seasonal herbs.

TOMATO SALAD WITH SPRING VEGETABLES, PESTO, AND BALSAMIC VINEGAR

La salade fraîcheur de tomate aux jeunes légumes printaniers, pistou de basilic et vinaigre balsamique

SERVES 6

6 poivrade artichokes, trimmed (small purple artichokes from Provence)

2 cups (500 ml) chicken stock

juice of half a lemon

6 ripe tomatoes, peeled and thinly sliced

12 cherry tomatoes, cut in half

2 cups (300 g) peas

2 cups (300 g) broad beans, peeled

6 green asparagus spears, sliced

6 baby carrots, peeled

6 cups (200 g) fresh young mesclun leaves

scant ½ cup (100 ml) olive oil

2 tablespoons (30 ml) balsamic vinegar

salt and freshly ground black pepper to taste

32 black olives, pitted (preferably Taggiascan, a small, fruity Italian olive)

balsamic vinegar to garnish

shaved Parmesan to garnish

For the basil pesto

1 clove of garlic, peeled and crushed

1 bunch of basil, chopped

1⅓ cups (300 ml) olive oil (preferably from Vallée des Baux)

Cook the artichokes in the chicken stock and lemon juice until cooked but still firm. Leave them in their liquid.

Cook the peas, beans, and asparagus briefly in a large quantity of salted water—they should remain crunchy. Drain and rinse with cold water. Do the same with the whole baby carrots.

Pesto

Mix the garlic with the basil, then add the olive oil. Keep chilled.

To serve

Arrange the sliced tomatoes and cherry tomatoes in a circle around the edge of a platter.

Dress the mesclun with a vinaigrette made with the olive oil and balsamic vinegar. Place the mesclun in the center of the circle of tomatoes.

Quarter the artichokes and season them. Season the other vegetables. Arrange the olives and vegetables, except for the asparagus and carrots, around the edge of the platter. Place the carrots and asparagus on the mesclun.

Dress the platter with balsamic vinegar, pesto, and shaved Parmesan.

The traditional cooking here in Provence comes from the peasants who cooked with ingredients from their own farms. They had their own chickens, rabbits, eggs, wheat to make their own bread, and grapes to make their own wine: they knew where their ingredients came from. It's not that they were better cooks but that their produce was their own.

Jean-André Charial

1½ cups (200 g) lardons

1 small onion, peeled and finely chopped

1 bouquet garni

1 clove of garlic, crushed

2 small (14–18 oz./400–500 g each) pigeons

3½ tablespoons (50 g) butter

generous ¾ cup (200 ml) water

1 heart of a lettuce, washed

3 cups (500 g) freshly picked peas, podded

12 baby carrots, scrubbed

pinch of Four Spice

salt and freshly ground black pepper to taste

FRENCH PIGEON

Pigeon à la française

Brown the lardons, onion, bouquet garni, and garlic in a cast-iron pan for 5 minutes. Set aside.

Brown the pigeons in the butter.

Add the water, lettuce, peas, baby carrots, spices, and lardon mixture you set aside earlier.

Season, cover, and cook for 10 minutes. Serve.

1 medium-sized rabbit, cut into 8 pieces

3 tablespoons olive oil

salt and freshly ground black pepper to taste

2 shallots, chopped

1 tablespoon flour

1 bottle (750 ml) white wine

2 lb. (1 kg) carrots, peeled and sliced in rounds

$\frac{1}{2}$ sprig of fresh thyme

2 bay leaves

RABBIT WITH CARROTS

Lapin aux carottes

Coat the rabbit pieces in olive oil and season to taste.

Put the rabbit and shallots in a cast-iron pan and cook gently for 2 minutes. Add the flour, stir, then pour in the white wine, so the meat is half covered. Cover, then simmer for 40 minutes, stirring occasionally.

Put the sliced carrots, thyme, and bay leaves in cold salted water. Bring to a boil; cook for 15 minutes.

Drain the carrots then add them to the rabbit, simmering over a gentle heat for a further 10 minutes. Serve.

The French peasant cuisine is at the basis of the culinary art. By this I mean it is composed of honest elements that *la grande cuisine* only embellishes.

Alexandre Dumaine

Light, refined, learned and noble, harmonious and orderly, clear and logical—the cooking of France is, in some strange manner, intimately linked to the genius of her greatest men.

Marcel Rouff

For the mushrooms

1 lb. (500 g) medium-sized cèpes (porcini mushrooms)

1 tablespoon olive oil (or duck fat)

salt and freshly ground black pepper to taste

For the veal kidneys

2 tablespoons (30 g) butter

4 veal kidneys, trimmed

$\frac{1}{2}$ tablespoon tarragon mustard

$\frac{1}{2}$ tablespoon green peppercorn mustard

$\frac{1}{2}$ tablespoon wholegrain mustard

$\frac{1}{2}$ glass Madeira wine, or a good port

salt and freshly ground black pepper to taste

VEAL KIDNEYS WITH PORCINI MUSHROOMS

Rognons de veau à la moutarde, cèpes à la bordelaise

Preheat the oven to 360°F (180°C).

Mushrooms

Clean the mushrooms with a damp cloth and trim the stalks, leaving about $\frac{1}{2}$ in. (1 cm) attached to each head. Thickly slice the mushrooms.

Put the olive oil in a non-stick pan then add the mushrooms, making sure that they are all in contact with the pan. Cook for 5 minutes on each side. Season.

Veal kidneys

Melt the butter in a pan until lightly browned, then add the kidneys. Cook for 3 or 4 minutes over a high heat until they are sealed but still tender. The longer they're cooked, the tougher they'll become. Bake in the oven for 10 minutes. Remove kidneys from the oven and let them rest on a plate to collect their juice.

Deglaze the pan with the Madeira, then add the mustard. Reduce by half.

Add the kidneys and their juice to the sauce, stirring so they are well coated, then serve immediately with the mushrooms.

Pétanque is played in towns and villages all over Provence. The origins of the game are thought to date back to the Egyptians and the ancient Greeks, and the Romans who are said to have introduced it to Provence first.
The modern version of the game was created in 1907 at the town of La Ciotat, where the first tournament was played in 1910. The steel *boules* commonly used today were first introduced in 1927.

Provençal cooking is based on garlic. The air in Provence is impregnated with the aroma of garlic, which makes it very healthful to breathe. Garlic is the main seasoning in bouillabaisse and in the principal sauces of the region. A sort of mayonnaise is made with it by crushing it in oil, and this is eaten with fish and snails. The lower classes in Provence often lunch on a crust of bread sprinkled with oil and rubbed with garlic.

Alexandre Dumas

The name **aïoli** (garlic mayonnaise) comes from the Provençal *alh* meaning garlic + *òli* meaning oil. There are as many recipes for it as there are families in Provence.

To make **aioli**, peel one whole bulb of garlic cloves and purée in a processor. Then add one cup of extra-virgin olive oil (or more if necessary) in a very thin stream until a smooth paste is achieved. Season with salt and lemon juice to taste.
Aioli is an ideal accompaniment to meat, fish, or vegetables or served on toasted bread. It is ideal as a base for flavored sauces, spreads, and mayonnaise.

Spices change your way of thinking and open your mind to flavor.

Jean-André Charial

POUR SALADE VERTE
COMPOSEE.............
25 GRS   5 EUROS
50 GRS   9 EUROS

4 shoulders of milk-fed lamb
(about 1 lb./550 g each)

fleur de sel (or coarse sea salt) to taste

8 sprigs of fresh thyme

4 cloves of garlic, crushed

scant ¼ cup (50 ml) olive oil

16 large stalks of fresh asparagus

1 bunch of wild asparagus

3½ tablespoons (50 g) butter

1⅓ cups (300 ml) lamb *jus*
(see recipe page 175)

salt and freshly ground black pepper
to taste

For the spice mix

5 teaspoons (10 g) Four Spice

6 cinnamon sticks (12 g)

10 teaspoons (30 g) ground black pepper

7 teaspoons (20 g) white cardamom
powder

1½ teaspoons (6 g) ground turmeric

10 teaspoons (20 g) powdered ginger

15 teaspoons (45 g) fennel seeds

MILK-FED LAMB SHOULDER WITH MILD SPICES

Epaule d'agneau de lait aux épices douces

Blend the spices for the spice mix in a blender and measure out 1 teaspoon per lamb shoulder.

Trim the fat from the lamb. Season with the salt and spice mix as above. Rub the meat with the thyme and the crushed garlic. Cook in the oven with the olive oil at 140°F (60°C) for 12 hours.

When the meat is ready, peel the fresh asparagus. Removing the woody ends, cut into even-sized pieces and tie in bundles of five. Cook in salted boiling water for 5 minutes.

Wash and trim the wild asparagus, leaving 1 in. (3 cm) of head. Cook in the salted boiling water for 30 seconds. Drain.

Foam the butter by heating in a pan until it froths, being careful not to burn it. Roll the wild asparagus in the foamed butter.

Season, and serve with the lamb and *jus*.

Identity is a living thing but tradition is just as important; so while there must always be change, we must also keep the spirit of tradition.

—

Lamb is a traditional Easter dish in France, when the first lambs of the season are ready.

Jean-André Charial

For the paste rub	2 teaspoons olive oil
1 sprig of fresh rosemary leaves (or 1 tablespoon dried rosemary)	1 tablespoon mustard
10 anchovy fillets in olive oil, drained	*For the meat*
3 cloves of garlic, peeled	2½ lb. (1.2 kg) leg of lamb
freshly ground black pepper to taste	4 cloves of garlic, unpeeled
2 teaspoons balsamic vinegar	

LEG OF LAMB RUBBED WITH ROSEMARY AND ANCHOVIES

Gigot d'agneau frotté au romarin et anchois

Paste rub

In a blender (in short bursts, scraping down the sides of the bowl when necessary) mix the rosemary, anchovies, garlic, pepper, vinegar, olive oil, and mustard until the mixture forms a paste that is not too smooth.

Lamb

Place the meat in an ovenproof dish and rub the paste into it, making sure to cover all sides. Cover with plastic wrap and refrigerate for at least an hour, preferably 3 to 4 hours.

Thirty minutes before cooking, take the meat from the refrigerator and rest it at room temperature.

Preheat the oven to 430°F (220°C). Remove the plastic wrap and place the unpeeled garlic under and around the meat.

Bake for 20 minutes, then lower the temperature to 265°F (130°C) and cook for a further 2½ hours, basting the meat every 30 minutes. If the meat is browning too quickly, cover it with aluminum foil.

Take the dish from the oven and if you have not already done so, cover it lightly in aluminum foil, and leave it to rest for at least 5 minutes.

To serve

Cut the meat at the table, serving it with the pan juices and a potato gratin.

Lamb cooked in pastry and served with dauphinois potatoes is a classic Oustau meal. It's what I cook for my family to show them that I love them.

Jean-André Charial

In the Mediterranean, feasting on lamb is a traditional means of ushering in the spring season. Sheep naturally lamb in March and April, hence the term "spring lamb."

LEGS OF LAMB IN A PASTRY CRUST

Gigot d'agneau en croute avec un tian d'aubergines, tomates et courgettes

SERVES 4

2 small legs of lamb
(less than 2 lb./1 kg each)

4 lamb kidneys, diced

2 tablespoons (30 g) butter

1 glass of Madeira wine, or a good port

several sprigs of fresh thyme and rosemary

salt and freshly ground black pepper to taste

10 $\frac{1}{2}$ oz. (300 g) pre-made puff pastry

1 egg yolk

lamb *jus* (see recipe on page 175)

For the tian

2 eggplants, cut in rounds

salt to cover

3 tablespoons (45 ml) olive oil

3 zucchini, sliced

3 onions, peeled and cut into rings

2 cloves of garlic, peeled and sliced

salt and freshly ground black pepper to taste

6 tomatoes, sliced and seasoned

1 teaspoon thyme flowers

1 teaspoon granulated sugar

Lamb

Preheat the oven to 480°F (250°C).

Bone the legs of lamb with a fine, sharp knife.

Cook the kidneys in a tablespoon of butter until brown. Deglaze the pan with the Madeira, then add the thyme and rosemary. Place this mixture in the cavities where the bones were removed from the lamb.

Reconstruct the leg of lamb, pulling the skin together and securing it with 2 or 3 stitches. Season with salt and pepper. Rub the legs of lamb with the remaining butter. Bake for about 15 minutes to seal the meat. Remove from the oven and set aside to cool for 10 minutes.

With a rolling pin, thinly roll out the pastry. Cut it in two triangular shapes, and fold a triangle of pastry around each lamb leg as you would a nappy on a baby. Brush with the egg yolk, put back in the oven, and cook for a further 10 minutes.

Cut the lamb into slices and serve with a lamb *jus*.

Tian

Preheat the oven to 300°F (150°C).

Put the eggplant rounds in a bowl and sprinkle them with salt. Leave to drain for an hour or so then pat dry.

Cook the eggplant in a frying pan for about 5 minutes in 2 tablespoons of oil. Replace them with the zucchini, onions, and garlic, and cook for 2 minutes. Season with salt and pepper.

Oil a gratin dish with the rest of the olive oil, then arrange the zucchini and eggplants, then the onions and tomatoes, in alternating rows. Sprinkle with thyme flowers and sugar. Bake in the oven for 35–40 minutes. Serve.

RACKS OF LAMB IN AN HERB CRUST

Carré d'agneau en croute d'herbes

SERVES 4

2 racks of lamb
(1¾ lb./800 g in total)

2½ cups (100 g) fresh parsley, chopped

2½ cups (100 g) fresh chervil, finely chopped

2 cloves of garlic, peeled and chopped

2 tablespoons breadcrumbs

1 tablespoon mustard

salt and freshly ground black pepper to taste

1½ tablespoons (25 g) butter, softened

fresh, chopped chives to garnish

For the lamb jus

9 oz. (250 g) lamb bones and trimmings

1 tablespoon (15 ml) olive oil

1 carrot, peeled and roughly diced

1 onion, peeled and roughly diced

1 small leek, sliced

⅓ cup (20 g) celeriac, chopped

4 cloves of garlic, unpeeled

1 tablespoon (15 ml) white wine

8½ cups (2 liters) water

1 cup (150 g) tomatoes, roughly diced

bouquet garni

Lamb jus

Brown the lamb bones and trimmings in the olive oil in a large pan over a high heat. Add the carrot, onion, leek, celeriac, and unpeeled cloves of garlic. Broil in the oven until brown.

Remove the pan from the oven, strain out the fat, deglaze the pan with the white wine, and place the pan on the stove top. Add the water, tomatoes, and the bouquet garni. Cook over a low heat until it has reduced by three-quarters.

Leave to rest, then strain and heat again until it has reduced by half. You should have 1 cup (250 ml) of *jus*. Refrigerate.

Racks of lamb

Preheat the oven to 430°F (220°C).

Bake the racks of seasoned lamb for 12 minutes. Remove from the oven and leave to rest.

In a bowl mix the herbs and the garlic with the breadcrumbs and mustard. Season with salt and pepper. Add the butter.

Cover the lamb in the herb mixture. Place in a baking dish and cook for 30 minutes.

Remove from the oven, cover with aluminum foil, and leave to rest for 10 minutes before serving.

To serve

While the lamb is resting, heat the *jus* on the stove top.

Sprinkle the lamb with chopped chives. Serve with the *jus* and an eggplant gratin (see recipe on page 176).

EGGPLANT GRATIN

Gratin d'aubergines

SERVES 6

For the tomatoes

$4\frac{1}{2}$ lb. (2 kg) tomatoes

4 tablespoons olive oil

3 cloves of garlic

1 onion, peeled and chopped

1 tablespoon tomato paste

1 tablespoon finely granulated sugar

salt and freshly ground black pepper to taste

3 sprigs of fresh parsley, chopped

1 small sprig of fresh thyme, chopped

1 bay leaf

$\frac{1}{2}$ bunch of fresh basil or tarragon leaves, chopped

For the gratin

4 eggplants, peeled and sliced lengthways

generous $\frac{3}{4}$ cup (200 ml) olive oil

1 bunch of fresh basil, chopped

scant $\frac{1}{2}$ cup (50 g) breadcrumbs

The crushed tomatoes and the eggplant can be prepared several hours in advance. The gratin, however, should be cooked immediately before serving.

Crushed tomatoes

To peel the tomatoes, cut a small cone from the base of each tomato with a sharp knife. Cut a small cross in the base, and plunge the tomatoes in boiling water for about 12 seconds, then in cold water for 15 seconds. The skin will just fall off. Slice the tomatoes lengthways, then with the knife remove the seeds and the pulp, leaving only the flesh.

In a cast-iron pan lightly cook the garlic in the olive oil. Add the chopped onion. Lightly cook (don't brown) then add the peeled tomatoes, tomato paste, sugar, salt, pepper, parsley, thyme, bay leaf, and basil or tarragon. Cover and cook for 1 hour over a low heat.

Gratin

In a large pan, fry the eggplant slices on both sides in the olive oil until they are golden brown. Work in batches, draining the cooked eggplant on paper towels as you go.

Brush the inside of a gratin dish with a further teaspoon of olive oil.

Put a thin layer of the tomatoes on the bottom of the gratin dish, then place a layer of the eggplant on top. Sprinkle with chopped basil. Form a second layer of tomatoes, followed by eggplant and basil, then a third of tomatoes. Sprinkle with breadcrumbs.

Turn the oven to full heat. Put a dish containing 1 in. (3 cm) of water in the oven. To prevent boiling, place a sheet of newspaper folded in half in the bottom of the dish.

Place the gratin dish in the bain-marie and bake for about 15 minutes.

Provençal Spring, 1903
Henry Herbert La Thangue (1859–1929)
La Thangue was a British painter who studied
in Paris and spent much of his time in Provence.

Daube Provençale is a stew made with
cubed beef braised in wine, vegetables,
garlic, and herbes de Provence. It may also
include olives, prunes, and flavoring with
duck fat, vinegar, brandy, lavender, nutmeg,
cinnamon, cloves, juniper berries, or orange
peel. For best results it is cooked in several
steps and cooled for a day between each
step to allow the flavors to combine. In the
Camargue, *daube* is sometimes made from
bulls killed in the bullfighting festivals.

Fortified towns are common in Provence and over seven hundred were built during the thirteenth and fourteenth centuries. Well-known fortified towns in Provence include Saint-Paul de Vence, Eze, and Les Baux de Provence.

5.

A meal should be
an unforgettable
experience.

Jean-André Charial

The secret of good cooking is
to make your guest feel as if
you have cooked his meal for
the first time, especially for
him, even if you have prepared
it a thousand times before.

Jean-André Charial

[To the French] *le Plaisir* is a part of the general fearless and joyful contact with life.

Edith Wharton

Bear in mind that you should conduct yourself in life as at a feast.

Epictetus

Something that is unique to France is the relationship between food and wine: the combination should be 1 + 1 = 3. The wine brings something to the dish and the dish brings something to the wine.

—

When you find the right wine to complement the food, magic happens.

Jean-André Charial

Each wine we tasted was accompanied by an imaginary menu, described with much lip-smacking and raising of the eyes to gastronomic heaven. We mentally consumed *écrevisses*, salmon cooked with sorrel, rosemary-garlic sauce, an *estouffade* of beef and olives, a *daube*, loin of pork spiked with slivers of truffle.

Peter Mayle

A good wine demonstrates the personality of the winemaker. Just as when you give the same ingredients to ten chefs, they create ten different dishes, wine is the same.

—

There are three elements to a good wine—the first is the soil, the second is the weather, the third is the man.

Jean-André Charial

How can anyone govern a nation that has 240 different kinds of cheese?

Charles de Gaulle

Chèvre chaud, literally "hot goat," is commonplace throughout Provence and is made by broiling goat's-milk cheese on bread. This is served on a mixed green salad and accompanied by a vinaigrette, olive oil, or balsamic vinegar.

Petit fours are small confections usually served at the end of a meal with coffee and can include small biscuits, meringues, macaroons, puff pastries, cakes, eclairs, and tartlets. The name comes from the French *petit four*, meaning "small oven," as they were traditionally made during the cooling process of coal-powered ovens in the eighteenth century, when coal was expensive and any heat generated, however small, needed to be utilized.

MILLEFEUILLE À LA BAUMANIÈRE

*Millefeuille, tradition
baumanière*

SERVES 6

For the puff pastry

$2\frac{1}{2}$ cups (250 g) flour

1 generous teaspoon (6 g) salt

1 tablespoon (15 g) butter, softened

scant $\frac{1}{2}$ cup (100 ml) cold water

$1\frac{3}{4}$ sticks (200 g) butter

confectioners' sugar for dusting

For the cream filling

1 cup (250 ml) milk

1 tablespoon (15 g) butter

1 vanilla pod

$\frac{1}{4}$ cup (50 g) granulated sugar

2 or 3 egg yolks

$\frac{1}{4}$ cup (25 g) flour

generous $\frac{3}{4}$ cup (200 ml) whipping cream

For the caramel ice cream

$1\frac{1}{4}$ cup (250 g) granulated sugar

scant $\frac{1}{2}$ cup (100 ml) cream

8 egg yolks (160 g), medium eggs, beaten

$\frac{1}{2}$ cup (125 ml) condensed milk

Puff pastry

Mix the flour, salt, and butter, add the cold water, then mix with your fingers until the dough is firm and smooth. Cover in plastic wrap and refrigerate for 4 hours.

Roll out the dough into a rectangle and place the butter in the center. Fold in the corners so the butter is wrapped in the dough, then roll out again until $1\frac{1}{4}$ in. (3 cm) thick. Fold in thirds and refrigerate for a further 2 hours. Repeat this four times—each time you will roll it out again and fold it in thirds.

When the pastry is ready, roll it out again—it should be about $\frac{1}{5}$ in. (5 mm) thick. Bake at 360°F (180°C) for about 10 minutes.

Remove from the oven, score in rectangles with a knife, sprinkle with confectioners' sugar, then return the pastry to the oven until the sugar caramelizes. Cut into rectangles.

Cream filling

In a saucepan bring the milk, butter, and vanilla pod to a boil. Beat together the sugar, egg yolks, and flour. When the milk comes to a boil, add some to the egg mixture, mix well, and return to the saucepan. Bring back to a boil, then remove from the heat and let cool. Whip the cream, add to the cooled mixture, and refrigerate.

Caramel ice cream

Caramelize the sugar—take care, as it burns easily. When caramelized, deglaze the pan with the cream. Add the beaten egg yolks, then cook as you would a custard. Add the condensed milk and process in an ice-cream maker.

Millefeuille

Assemble the millefeuille by layering the rectangles of puff pastry with the cream filling. Serve with the caramel ice cream.

CHOCOLATE MOUSSE WITH COCOA-BEAN BRITTLE AND CARAMEL ICE CREAM

Mousseux au chocolat Grand Cru, craquant au grué de cacao, crème glacée au caramel

SERVES 5

For the chocolate froth

1½ (3.75 g) gelatin sheets

1 cup (250 ml) milk

3½ oz. (100 g) dark chocolate

For the chocolate mousse

½ (1.25 g) gelatin sheet

scant ½ cup (110 ml) whipping cream, 30 percent fat content

6 oz. (175 g) dark chocolate, grated (preferably Grand Cru)

4 or 5 egg whites

¼ cup (50 g) granulated sugar

5 ladyfingers, broken in half, dipped in coffee

scant ½ cup (100 ml) strong black coffee

For the cocoa-bean brittle

⅓ cup (30 g) flour

⅔ cup (125 g) granulated sugar

2 oz. (60 g) cocoa beans, crushed

scant ¼ cup (50 ml) orange juice

3½ tablespoons (50 g) butter, melted

caramel ice cream

Chocolate froth

Soak the gelatin in iced water for 20 minutes. Bring the milk to a boil, then add the gelatin. Break the chocolate into a bowl, pour the mixture on top, and blend until frothy. Refrigerate overnight.

Chocolate mousse

Soak the gelatin in iced water for 20 minutes.

Bring the cream to a boil, melt the gelatin into it, then add to the chocolate in a large bowl. Mix together and let the mixture cool.

Beat the egg whites together with the sugar until they form soft peaks.

Gently blend the two mixtures, being careful not to collapse the beaten egg whites.

Divide the mixture into five glasses, placing half a coffee-soaked ladyfinger in the bottom of each glass. Fill half of the glass with mousse, then top with the other half of the ladyfinger.

Refrigerate for 2 hours.

Cocoa-bean brittle

Mix together all the cold ingredients, then carefully add the melted butter. Chill for 1 hour.

Spread on a baking sheet and cook at 360°F–390°F (180°C–200°C) for 8–10 minutes.

When cooled, break into tiles.

To serve

Pour the chocolate froth into the glasses, on top of the mousse and ladyfingers.

Place a tile of brittle on top of each mousse, along with a scoop of caramel ice cream.

Even the *coeur flottant merveilleux aux fraises*, presented with a great flourish, made little impression, for it was no more than what may happen to the simple, honest dish of strawberries and cream once it falls into the hands of a Frenchman.

Doctor Watson, in *Sherlock Holmes and the Hapsburg Tiara*

12 strawberries, halved

For the strawberry sorbet

1 lb. (500 g) strawberries, puréed

scant $\frac{1}{2}$ cup (100 ml) water

For the hazelnut crumble

7 tablespoons (80 g) granulated sugar

$\frac{1}{2}$ cup (50 g) flour

juice of 1 lemon

$\frac{1}{4}$ cup (50 g) granulated sugar

$3\frac{1}{2}$ tablespoons (50 g) butter

generous $\frac{1}{2}$ cup (50 g) ground hazelnuts

HAZELNUT CRUMBLE WITH STRAWBERRY SORBET

Crumble gourmand au goût de fraises d'ici

Crumble

Put all the ingredients in a bowl and rub gently with your fingertips until the mixture resembles breadcrumbs. Spread the crumble on a baking tray and bake at 340°F (170°C) until crisp.

Sorbet

Purée the fresh strawberries. Add the water and the sugar and bring to a boil. Add the lemon juice. Blend together, then process in an ice-cream maker.

To serve

Serve the dessert in individual bowls (or glasses), with the crumble at the bottom, then the sorbet and halved fruit on top.

MELON SORBET, RASPBERRIES, AND LIME MERINGUES

Cristalline gourmande melon et fraise, blanc manger aux zestes de citron vert

SERVES 6

24 raspberries

For the melon balls

1 to 2 melons

$\frac{1}{2}$ cup (100 g) granulated sugar

1 cup (250 ml) boiling water

For the meringues

3 egg whites

$\frac{1}{4}$ cup (50 g) granulated sugar

1 vanilla pod

zest of 1 lime

For the melon sorbet

scant $\frac{1}{2}$ cup (100 ml) water

$\frac{1}{2}$ cup (100 g) granulated sugar

1 lb. (500 g) melon, chopped and puréed

1 tablespoon Muscat (or dessert wine)

For the caramel arlette

$\frac{3}{4}$ cup (100 g) confectioners' sugar

4 teaspoons (20 ml) water

$3\frac{1}{2}$ oz. (100 g) puff pastry

Melon balls

Make the melon balls using a melon baller or a teaspoon. Make the syrup by dissolving the sugar in the water, stirring constantly. Once the sugar is dissolved completely, pour the hot syrup over the melon balls to poach them. Cool.

Meringues

Beat together the egg whites, sugar, and vanilla to form a firm meringue. Form small balls out of the mixture, place on a plate covered in plastic wrap, and top with lime zest.

Cook in the microwave on full power for 20 seconds.

Leave to cool in the refrigerator for 10 minutes.

Melon sorbet

Boil the water and sugar, add the melon and Muscat and process in an ice-cream maker.

Caramel arlette

Blend the confectioners' sugar and water. Roll out the pastry thinly on to baking paper, glaze with the sugar mixture. Bake at 360°F (180°C) until lightly browned. Cool.

To serve

Serve in a glass, layering first the sorbet, then the melon balls, raspberries, the meringues, and finally the *arlette*.

$\frac{1}{2}$ cup (100 g) granulated sugar

generous $\frac{3}{4}$ cup (70 g) ground hazelnuts

$1\frac{3}{4}$ tablespoons (10 g) cake flour

2 large or 3 small eggs

3 egg yolks

1 cup (250 ml) whipping cream,
30 percent fat content

4–5 cups (500 g) cherries
(leave the stones in to retain their flavor)

raspberries to garnish

fresh cherries to garnish

confectioners' sugar to garnish

almond or pistachio ice cream to serve

HAZELNUT CLAFOUTIS WITH CHERRIES AND RASPBERRIES

Clafoutis noisette aux fruits de saison, cerises et framboises

Preheat the oven to 360°F (180°C).

Mix all of the dry ingredients together. Gradually stir in the eggs and egg yolks, then the cream.

Divide the batter among 4 or 5 small ovenproof dishes and bake in the oven for 2 minutes.

Remove from the oven, place a layer of cherries on top, and bake for a further 20 minutes.

Remove from the oven again, garnish with raspberries, fresh cherries, and confectioners' sugar.

Serve immediately with the ice cream.

Ice cream is exquisite. What a pity it isn't illegal.

Voltaire

The first French recipes for flavored ices appeared in 1674, in Nicolas Lémery's *Recueil de curiositéz rares et nouvelles de plus admirables effets de la nature* and in François Massialot's 1692 edition of *Nouvelle Instruction pour les Confitures, les Liqueurs, et les Fruits*.

Pastis ... the milk of Provence.

Pastis is a charming drink—the first glass invites the second, and very often the second invites the third. But be careful, very careful, it is insidious. Before you know it you may need help to walk, unless you are a Provençal.

Hrayr Berberoglu

Pastis is the traditional liqueur of Provence, flavored with anise and typically up to 45 percent alcohol by volume. When absinthe was banned in France in 1915, the major absinthe producers (then Pernod Fils and Ricard) created pastis.

This new drink was made without the banned wormwood and with more aniseed flavor, sugar, and a lower alcohol content. It is usually served diluted with water, which turns it a cloudy color. It is very popular in Marseille.

Advertising poster for the Marseilles-based Absinthe Picardine, circa 1900

Everything ends this way in France—everything. Weddings, christenings, duels, burials, swindlings, diplomatic affairs— everything is a pretext for a good dinner.

Jean Anouilh

Café Terrace, Place du Forum, Arles, 1888
Vincent van Gogh (1853–1890)

AFTERWORD
Rachael McKenna

Photographing images for *Lunch in Provence* has been an amazing experience for my family and me. Not only have we had the pleasure of sampling some of the most exquisite dishes we have ever eaten, but we have spent many happy hours wandering around quaint villages and Provençal cities, sampling market produce, and experiencing the atmosphere of each place we visited. We have physically, emotionally, and mentally fallen in love with life in Provence.

As a photographer, working in Provence is a delight: whatever the time of day or whatever the subject, each image explodes with color and character. The light is magical at all hours of the day and depending on my chosen angle I can be treated with a rich and luminous light, or one that is soft and hazy. Either way, it is hard not to create images that breathe romanticism. You can visit the same place day after day and find something new to capture through your lens each time—whether it is the character of the people and animals on the streets, the weathered paint on the shutters that frame the windows of the houses, or the aged stone of the engraved sign etched into the wall outside a café. Each time I press the shutter I can almost hear my camera sigh with pleasure.

And it's not only my camera that seems to be happy; my husband Andy, my daughter Charlize, and I love every minute we spend in Provence. Surrounded by friends and family with a glass of chilled rosé in hand, a gentle breeze slightly cooling the air that's been heated by a baking sun, and an atmosphere that is filled with smiles and laughter, life is indeed wonderful. I am in heaven to be surrounded by such beauty, and Andy is at his happiest sourcing fresh, daily produce from the local markets. Inspired by the days spent photographing the culinary delights served to us at Jean-André Charial's exquisite restaurants, Andy spoils us with his own tasteful masterpieces, our afternoons spent lunching in the sun completed by another beautiful sunset.

I feel at home here and, while my heart will always belong to New Zealand, for the time being Provence has taken a firm grasp of my soul. I hope you, too, have enjoyed this small yet delicious slice of Provençal life.

Rachael and Andy's daughter, Charlize, enjoys dessert on location at Oustau de Baumanière, Les Baux de Provence.

I love Provence. I work every day because I love to be here and to cook for people, to see them happy and to see their eyes light up.

Jean-André Charial

Jean-André Charial embodies the spirit of lunch in Provence; the act of sharing a meal with loved ones, of being at one with your environment and, by extension, the food that comes from your environment that you create for, and share with, those closest to you. Lunch, he says, is the most important meal of the day, and is one he never misses. Always lunch, always with his wife Geneviève, and always with a glass of wine.

Oustau de Baumanière, nestled in a remote corner of the Alpilles in the Val d'Enfer (Hell's Valley, which inspired Dante), is a gastronomic oasis and a homage to Provençal cuisine. Its motto, "belles manières, art de vivre et d'accueillir êtres et choses avec un sens aigu du bonheur," or

"beautiful manners, the art of living and of welcoming every-thing and everyone with an acute sense of happiness," sums up Jean-André's approach to life and it is with this firmly in mind that he and Geneviève welcome friends, family, and guests to their establishments in Les Baux de Provence, considered by many to be the very heart of Provence.

Established by Jean-André's grandfather Raymond Thuilier in 1945, the same year that Jean-André was born, Oustau de Baumanière was little more than an abandoned sixteenth-century farmhouse. Inspired by his mother, who he watched cook at a train station café in Privas in the Ardèche when growing up, Raymond quickly established Oustau as a culinary tour de

force that was awarded its first Michelin star in 1949, its second in 1952, and its third in 1954.

Jean-André started working with his grandfather in the kitchens at Oustau in 1972, and assumed complete responsibility upon Raymond's death in 1993. He is passionate about the quality of food and a strong advocate of biodynamic practices, establishing an organic kitchen garden in 2003, which is officially certified organic by France's ECOCERT. "A holistic approach to the body starts with knowing where food comes from and how it's been grown. Healthy insects make healthy plants, which in turn make healthy animals, which then make healthy humans. If you protect the earth it is better for everybody," he says. The garden

provides the chefs of Oustau de Baumanière and La Cabro d'Or, Oustau's sister establishment in the Val d'Enfer, with produce and herbs that they cannot find at local markets, and is guarded on all sides by La Cabro d'Or's goats.

Following this holistic approach to cuisine, Jean-André also creates his own wine cultivating grapevines using biodynamic practices to produce grape varieties that "truly reflect their *terroir*—their home ground. I like the idea that when the roots develop and go down into the soil, their bounty provides an expression of this part of the earth. All produce is an expression of the soil and so when you are cooking, the better the produce you use, the better your cooking will be, and the better the grapes you have, the better your wine will be."

Visited by the great and the good, the rich and the famous, gourmets and travelers alike, Oustau has long been a favorite destination for people from all walks of life, drawn not only by the food of Oustau, but also the light, beauty, and romance of Provence. From Georges Pompidou, Charles de Gaulle, François Mitterand, and Jacques Chirac to John F. Kennedy and Gerald Ford; from Prince Rainier and Princess Grace to Britain's Queen Mother; from Pablo Picasso to Jean Cocteau; from Jean Reno and Luciano Pavarotti to Bono; from James Coburn to Hugh Grant, and the list goes on.

Perhaps, however, French writer James de Coquet's observation following Queen Elizabeth II's state visit in 1972 sums up Oustau best: "I am happy for the Queen of England. In the kaleidoscope of memories that her stay in France will form, one image will stand out from the red carpets, the drawn sabers, the marble surroundings and the official smiles—one very simple and highly poetic image: that of a small red snapper served in a broth, wreathed with basil."

Jean-André puts it more simply: "Eating good food and drinking good wine with someone you love is perfection."

Bon appétit.

Oustau de Baumanière
Les Baux de Provence

Jean-André Charial
Owner

Sylvestre Wahid
Chef de Cuisine

Jonathan Wahid
Pastry Chef

Bernard Chatton
Chef

The majority of the recipes featured in *Lunch in Provence* were created by Jean-André Charial and his team of chefs at Les Maisons de Baumanière: Oustau de Baumanière, La Cabro d'Or, La Prieuré, and La Place.

Recipes

Red mullet with grapefruit, 75; Stuffed zucchini flowers, 78; Green and white asparagus with morels, 107; Millefeuille à la Baumanière, 203; Melon sorbet, raspberries, and lime meringues, 210.

The chefs at Oustau de Baumanière also created the traditional Provençal dishes included here.

Ratatouille Niçoise, 82; Artichoke barigoule, 88; Mussel gratin, 123; Bouillabaisse, 126–7; Scorpionfish with vegetable stuffing, 129; Tomatoes and mozzarella, 144; French pigeon, 150; Rabbit with carrots, 153; Veal kidneys with porcini mushrooms, 157; Leg of lamb rubbed with rosemary and anchovies, 168; Legs of lamb in a pastry crust, 173; Racks of lamb in an herb crust, 175; Eggplant gratin, 176; Hazelnut clafoutis with cherries and raspberries, 212.

La Prieuré
Villeneuve-lès-Avignon

Fabien Fage
Chef de Cuisine

Built in 1322, La Prieuré was a priory for Chanoine monks and became a family residence for painters after the French Revolution. It was converted into a hotel in 1943 and was reopened by Jean-André and Geneviève Charial in 2007.

Recipe

Asparagus with slow-cooked eggs, mushrooms, and truffles, 94.

La Cabro d'Or
Les Baux de Provence

Michel Hulin
Chef de Cuisine

La Cabro d'Or, which means "the golden goat," takes its name from a verse of the poem *Mireille* by renowned Provençal poet Frédéric Mistral: "The Golden Goat, which no mortal can milk or own. / Under the rocks of Baumanière licks the moss from the stone." Situated at the base of the Alpilles in the Val d'Enfer, La Cabro d'Or was originally opened by Raymond Thuilier as a country inn for horseback riders but quickly outgrew its status as Oustau's "little brother," earning its own Michelin star.

Recipes
Red mullet with spring vegetables, pesto, croutons, and tapenade, 68; Sea bass on roasted risotto cakes with calamari, fennel, chorizo, zucchini, and slow-roasted tomato sauce, 120–1; Tomato salad with spring vegetables, pesto, and balsamic vinegar, 147; Chocolate mousse with cocoa-bean brittle and caramel ice cream, 204.

La Place
Maussane-les-Alpilles

Fanny Rey
Chef de Cuisine

A bistro installed in a two-storied house on the main square of the village of Maussane-les-Alpilles, La Place was opened in 2005 to serve simple yet gourmet dishes from the region.

Recipes
Provençal vegetables with pesto, 66; Grilled sea bass with ratatouille, 85; Purple artichokes with chorizo and crushed olives, 91; Milk-fed lamb shoulder with mild spices, 165; Hazelnut crumble with strawberry sorbet, 209; Lemon tarts, 109.

For more information on Les Maisons de Baumanière visit www.maisonsdebaumaniere.com

GOURMET INDEX

IMAGE CREDITS

Front cover and spine: Oustau de Baumanière; back cover, from left to right: Gordes, Vaucluse; Oustau; Sault, Vaucluse; Oustau; endpapers: Cassis, Bouches-du-Rhône; pp. 2–3: Oustau; p. 4: La Cabro d'Or; p. 6: Bistrot des Philosophes, Aix-en-Provence, Bouches-du-Rhône; p. 9: Oustau; p. 10: top, left: Villefranche-sur-Mer, Alpes-Maritimes; top, right: Gourdon, Alpes-Maritimes; center, left: Château des Alpilles; center: Vieux-Nice, Alpes-Maritimes; center, right: figs; bottom, left: Les Baux de Provence, Bouches-du-Rhône; bottom, right: Villefranche-sur-Mer, Alpes-Maritimes; p. 13: top, left: Lieuran-lès-Béziers, Hérault; top, right: Café du Roi René, Aix-en-Provence, Bouches-du-Rhône; bottom, both: Aix-en-Provence, Bouches-du-Rhône; p. 14, Café de la Place, Eygalières, Bouches-du-Rhône; p. 17: view from Château de la Chèvre d'Or, Eze, Alpes-Maritimes; p. 18: top, left: Hôtel Crillon le Brave; top, right: Vieux-Nice, Alpes-Maritimes; bottom, left: Nice, Alpes-Maritimes; bottom, right: Château de la Chèvre d'Or, Eze, Alpes-Maritimes; p. 21: Oustau; p. 22: top, left: Saint-Paul de Vence, Alpes-Maritimes; top, right: Aix-en-Provence, Bouches-du-Rhône; bottom, left: Oustau; bottom, right: Château des Alpilles; p. 25: Gourdon, Alpes-Maritimes; p. 26: top, left: Château de Beauregard; top, right: Gourdon, Alpes-Maritimes; bottom, left: Café de la Place, Eygalières, Bouches-du-Rhône; bottom, right: Château de Beauregard; p. 28: Aix-en-Provence, Bouches-du-Rhône; p. 29: Grasse, Alpes-Maritimes; pp. 30–1: Aix-en-Provence, Bouches-du-Rhône; p. 32: Le Manoir, Maisons de Baumanière, Les Baux de Provence, Bouches-du-Rhône; pp. 34–5: Sault, Vaucluse; p. 36: left: Sault, Vaucluse; center and right: Vieux-Nice, Alpes-Maritimes; pp. 37–41: Sault, Vaucluse; p. 42: left: Bechard boulangerie and pâtisserie, Aix-en-Provence, Bouches-du-Rhône; right: Pissaladière, Oustau; p. 43: Cassis, Bouches-du-Rhône; p. 44: Vieux-Nice, Alpes-Maritimes; p. 45: top: Oustau; bottom, left: Vieux-Nice, Alpes-Maritimes; bottom, right: Oustau; pp. 46–7: Hôtel Crillon-le-Brave; p. 49: Gordes, Vaucluse; p. 50: top, left and right: Vieux-Nice, Alpes-Maritimes; bottom, left: Aix-en-Provence, Bouches-du-Rhône; bottom, right: Grasse, Alpes-Maritimes; p. 52: Aix-en-Provence, Bouches-du-Rhône; pp. 54–5: Rousillon, Vaucluse; p. 56: top, left: La Cabro d'Or; top, right: Château de la Chèvre d'Or; bottom, left: Le Mas des Songes; bottom, right: Saint-Rémy-de-Provence, Alpes-Maritimes;

pp. 58–9: organic vineyard, Domaine de Lauzières, Mouriès, Bouches-du-Rhône; pp. 60–3: organic vegetable gardens, Maisons de Baumanière; p. 64: Soupe au pistou, Oustau; p. 65 top, left, right, and bottom, left: organic vegetable garden, Maisons de Baumanière; bottom, right: Oliviers & Co, Aix-en-Provence, Bouches-du-Rhône; p. 67: La Place; p. 69: La Cabro d'Or; p. 70, both: L'Isle-sur-la-Sorgue, Vaucluse; pp. 72–6, Oustau; p. 77, all: Nice, Alpes-Maritimes and Aix-en-Provence, Bouches-du-Rhône; p. 79: Oustau; p. 80: Nice, Alpes-Maritimes; p. 81: Organic vegetable garden, Maisons de Baumanière; p. 83: Oustau de Baumanière; p. 84: La Place; p. 86: Aix-en-Provence, Bouches-du-Rhône; p. 87: top, left: marché paysan (farmers market), Coustellet, Vaucluse; top, right: Oustau; bottom: Vieux-Nice, Alpes-Maritimes; p. 89: Oustau; p. 90: La Place; pp. 92–3: Franck and Mirette, La Truffe du Ventoux; p. 95: Le Prieuré; p. 96: Oustau; p. 99: road between Les Baux de Provence and Eygalières, Bouches-du-Rhône; p. 100: Maussane-les-Alpilles to Mouriès, Bouches-du-Rhône; p. 102: Maussane-les-Alpilles, Bouches-du-Rhône; p. 104: top: Vieux-Nice, Alpes-Maritimes; bottom: Les Baux de Provence, Bouches-du-Rhône; p. 106: Oustau; p. 108: La Place; pp. 110–1: Cassis, Bouches-du-Rhône; p. 112: Cannes, Alpes-Maritimes; p. 113: Villefranche-sur-Mer, Alpes-Maritimes; p. 114: top, left: Beau Rivage, Nice, Alpes-Maritimes; top, right: Saint-Jean-Cap-Ferrat, Alpes-Maritimes; center, left: Cassis, Bouches-du-Rhône; center: Hôtel Beau Rivage, Nice, Alpes-Maritimes; center, right: Saint-Jean-Cap-Ferrat, Alpes-Maritimes; bottom, left: Cannes, Alpes-Maritimes; bottom, right: Calanque de Port-Milou, Cassis, Bouches-du-Rhône; p. 116: Villefranche-sur-Mer, Alpes-Maritimes; p. 117: Lunch in Aix-en-Provence, Bouches-du-Rhône; p. 118: top, left: Villefranche-sur-Mer, Alpes-Maritimes; top, right: Oustau; bottom, left: Cassis, Bouches-du-Rhône; bottom, right: local fisherman Jean Paul, Villefranche-sur-Mer, Alpes-Maritimes; p. 119: Vieux-Nice, Alpes-Maritimes; p. 121: La Cabro d'Or; p. 122: Oustau; p. 124: top, left: La Poissonnerie, Cassis, Bouches-du-Rhône; top, right: Cassis, Bouches-du-Rhône; bottom, left: Aix-en-Provence, Bouches-du-Rhône; bottom, right: Cassis, Bouches-du-Rhône; pp. 127–8: Oustau; p. 130: Maussane-les-Alpilles, Bouches-du-Rhône; p. 133: Le Prieuré; p. 134: Les Baux de Provence, Bouches-du-Rhône; p. 136: Saint-Paul de Vence, Alpes-Maritimes; p. 137: Oustau; p. 138: Cassis, Bouches-du-Rhône; p. 139: top, left: Les Baux de Provence, Bouches-du-Rhône; top, right: Arles, Bouches-du-Rhône; bottom, left: Vieux-Nice, Alpes-Maritimes; bottom, right: olive harvesting, Maussane-les-Alpilles, Bouches-du-Rhône; p. 140: left: La Place; right: olive harvesting, Maussane-les-Alpilles, Bouches-du-Rhône; p. 141: Niçoise salad; p. 142: Aix-en-Provence, Bouches-du-Rhône; p. 145: Oustau; p. 146: La Cabro d'Or; p. 148: Aix-en-Provence, Bouches-du-Rhône; pp. 151–2: Oustau; p. 154: tuna, Hôtel Belles Rives; p. 155: top, left: Saint-Rémy-de-Provence, Alpes Maritimes; top, right: Charles Gasiglia, boucherie La Marseillaise, Villefranche-sur-Mer, Alpes-Maritimes; bottom, left: boucherie, Vieux-Nice, Alpes-Maritimes; bottom, right: Le Prieuré; p. 156: Oustau; p. 158: Saint-Paul de Vence, Alpes-Maritime; p. 159: both: Saint-Paul de Vence, Alpes-Maritime; p. 160: Vieux-Nice, Alpes-Maritimes; p. 161: Les Baux de Provence, Bouches-du-Rhône; p. 162: top, left: Vieux-Nice, Alpes-Maritimes; top, right and bottom: Aix-en-Provence, Bouches-du-Rhône; p. 163: left: Vieux-Nice, Alpes-Maritimes: right: Vieux-Nice, Alpes-Maritimes; p. 164: La Place; p. 166: Maisons de Baumanière; p. 169: Oustau; p. 170: La Cabro d'Or; p. 171: top, left: Charlize, Aix-en-Provence, Bouches-du-Rhône; top, right: Le Prieuré; bottom, left: Oustau; bottom, right: Café, L'Isle-sur-la-Sorgue, Vaucluse; pp. 172–7: Oustau; p. 178: top: Vallée Loire; bottom, left: Oustau; bottom, right: Daube Provençal; p. 180: Gordes, Vaucluse;

p. 181: top, left: Villefranche-sur-Mer, Alpes-Maritimes; top, right: Saint-Paul de Vence, Alpes-Maritimes; bottom, left: Villefranche-sur-Mer, Alpes-Maritimes; bottom, right: Gordes, Vaucluse; pp. 182–3: Gourdon, Alpes-Maritimes; p. 185: Aix-en-Provence, Bouches-du-Rhône; p. 186: Château de la Chèvre d'Or; p. 188: top, left: Aix-en-Provence, Bouches-du-Rhône; top, right: Café, L'Isle-sur-la-Sorgue, Vaucluse; center, left: Hôtel Crillon-le-Brave; center and center, right: Oustau; bottom, left: Nice, Alpes-Maritimes; bottom, right: Château de la Chèvre d'Or; p. 189; Aix-en-Provence, Bouches-du-Rhône; p. 190: Oustau; p. 192; Château de la Chèvre d'Or; p. 193: Oustau; pp. 194–6: organic vineyard, Domaine de Lauzières, Mouriès, Bouches-du-Rhône; p. 198: top, left: Cabris, Alpes-Maritimes; top, right: Cassis, Bouches-du-Rhône; bottom, left: Oustau; bottom, right: Cassis, Bouches-du-Rhône; p. 199: fromage de chèvre (goat-milk cheese), Domaine du Pierredon, Mouriès, Bouches-du-Rhône; p. 200: left: Chez Jo, Aix-en-Provence, Bouches-du-Rhône; right: Oustau; p. 201: Bechard boulangerie and pâtisserie, Aix-en-Provence, Bouches-du-Rhône; p. 202: Oustau; p. 205: La Cabro d'Or; p. 207: top, left: Saint-Rémy-de-Provence, Alpes Maritimes; top, right: La Cabro d'Or; bottom, left: La Cabro d'Or; bottom, right: petit fours, Oustau; p. 208: La Place; p. 211: Oustau; p. 213: Oustau; pp. 214–5: La Vallée des Baux de Provence, Bouches-du-Rhône; pp. 216–7: Barbarac, créateur de glaces, Cannes, Alpes-Maritimes; p. 219: top, left: Vieux-Nice, Alpes-Maritimes; top, right: Vieux-Nice, Alpes-Maritimes; bottom, left: Vieux-Nice, Alpes-Maritimes; bottom, right: pastis, Vieux-Nice, Alpes-Maritimes; pp. 220–3: Villefranche-sur-Mer, Alpes-Maritimes; p 224: Les Baux de Provence, Bouches-du-Rhône; p. 225: Charlize, La Guigou, Oustau; p. 226: Jean-André Charial, at the entrance to the restaurant at Oustau; p. 227: left: Oustau sits beneath the rocks of Les Alpilles; right: A view across the fields to Les Alpilles.

Châteaux, Restaurants, and Hotels

Les Maisons de Baumanière
 www.maisonsdebaumaniere.com
Oustau de Baumanière, Les Baux de Provence, Bouches-du-Rhône
 www.oustaudebaumaniere.com
La Cabro d'Or, Les Baux de Provence, Bouches-du-Rhône
 www.lacabrodor.com
Le Prieuré, Villeneuve-lès-Avignon, Gard
 www.leprieure.com
La Place, Maussane des Alpilles, Bouches-du-Rhône
 www.maisonsdebaumaniere.com
Le Mas des Songes, Monteux, Vaucluse
 www.masdessonges.com
Hôtel Crillon-le-Brave, Crillon-le-Brave, Vaucluse
 www.crillonlebrave.com
La Truffe du Ventoux, Monteux, Vaucluse
 www.truffes-ventoux.com
Hôtel Belles Rives, Juan-les-Pins, Alpes-Maritime
 www.bellesrives.com
Carlton, Cannes, Alpes-Maritimes
 www.intercontinental.com
Hôtel Beau Rivage, Nice, Alpes-Maritimes
 www.hotelnicebeaurivage.com
Château de la Chèvre d'Or, Eze, Alpes-Maritimes
 www.chevredor.com
Château des Alpilles, Saint-Rémy-de-Provence, Alpes-Maritimes
 www.chateaudesalpilles.com
Château de Beauregard, Jonquières, Vaucluse
 www.chateaubeauregard.com

ACKNOWLEDGMENTS
Rachael McKenna

While this has been one of the most challenging projects I've ever done as a photographer, it has also been one of the most fulfilling.

As always, my most heartfelt thanks go to my husband Andy and our daughter Charlize, I couldn't have done this without you. It's not easy being on the road for months on end, but you are both always there beside me, smiling your encouragement. Andy, this project is as much yours as mine and you can be proud that dishes you prepared sit alongside meals created by Provence's finest.

To my publishers Geoff Blackwell and Ruth Hobday at PQ Blackwell for giving me this extraordinary opportunity to explore new areas. The creative process has been incredibly rewarding and when I look at these pages my smile lights up the room. Thank you for your perseverance and belief in me.

It has been an incredible honor to work with Jean-André Charial. Never before have I tasted such exquisite food, received such faultless service, and worked in such a beautiful environment. Thank you for your patience, generosity, and assistance in the creation of this book.

To the team at Les Maisons de Baumanière: Chef de Cuisine Sylvestre Wahid and his team of talented chefs at Oustau de Baumanière were incredible, and special thanks to chef Bernard Chatton and sous-chef Gary Kirchens for preparing the dishes featured in the book. Thanks also to Phillip, the waiting staff, and sommeliers at Oustau for making us feel so welcome while we were on location. The masterpieces created by Michel Hulin, Chef de Cuisine at La Cabro d'Or, were exquisite—it was a delight to photograph your creations. To Fabien Fage, Chef de Cuisine at Le Prieuré, for his artistic creations—some of my favorite images are of your beautiful plates. And thanks to Fanny Rey, Chef de Cuisine at La Place, for treating me to such delicious flavors.

I also had the pleasure of working with many other restaurants, cafés, and hotels in Provence. Not all of them feature in the book, but I am grateful for their cooperation. In particular I would like to thank the following establishments: Château de la Chèvre d'Or, Eze; Hôtel Crillon le Brave, near Avignon; Château des Alpilles, Saint-Rémy-de-Provence; Hôtel Belles Rives, Juan-les-Pins; Carlton Cannes; Hôtel Beau Rivage, Nice; Barbarac, créateur de glaces, Cannes.

A big thank-you to Patricia Wells for your introduction, and for sharing your knowledge, experiences, and culinary adventures. Your words are an inspiration and a delight.

I am also extremely grateful to the people of Provence: not only is it a region of stunning landscapes but every person I approached was kind, generous, and friendly, and it's a place I would be proud to call home.

Last, but not least, I would like to thank my family: Andy's parents, Carol and Howard McKenna, it has been wonderful to share some of our Provençal experiences with you; to my mum, dad, and twin sister Becks, I wish you had been able to experience our amazing journey through Provence—hopefully you will one day very soon!

Salut Provence, you are truly a place worth visiting for more than just lunch!

À bientôt.

Recipes translated from the French by Linda Burgess and Lisette du Plessis
Additional text and editorial coordination: Ruth Hobday
Design: www.inhousedesign.co.nz
Additional typesetting: Sarah Anderson and Helene Dehmer
Printed in China by 1010 Printing International Limited

Produced and originated by PQ Blackwell Limited
116 Symonds Street, Auckland 1010, New Zealand
www.pqblackwell.com
Concept and design copyright © 2012 PQ Blackwell Limited
Images copyright © 2012 Rachael Hale Trust
www.rachaelmckenna.com
Introduction copyright © 2012 Patricia Wells Ltd
Recipes copyright © Jean-André Charial

All images by Rachael McKenna except pages 53, 101, 105, 115, 179, 218, and 221 courtesy Getty images.

Quotations from: p. 28: Nicola Williams and Catherine Le Nevez reproduced with permission from *Provence & the Côte d'Azur*, ed. 6 © 2010 Lonely Planet; p. 36: Sara Clemence reprinted by permission of Forbes Media LLC © 2011; p. 46: Somerset Maugham from *The Razor's Edge*, reproduced with permission of A. P. Watt Limited on behalf of the Royal Literary Fund; p. 53: Keith Floyd reprinted by permission of HarperCollins Publishers Limited © 1989 Keith Floyd; p. 57: Bonnie Manion reproduced with permission of the author, www.VintageGardenGal.com, a garden lifestyle blog; pp. 51 and 218: Hrayr Berberoglu reproduced with permission of the author; pp. 131 and 136: Lawrence Durrell reproduced with permission of Curtis Brown Group Ltd, London, on behalf of the Estate of Lawrence Durrell, copyright © the Estate of Lawrence Durrell, 1945; p. 136: Mark R. Vogel reproduced with permission of the author; p. 193: Peter Mayle from *A Year in Provence*, illustrated by Judith Clancy (Hamish Hamilton 1989, Penguin Books 2000), copyright © Peter Mayle, 1989; p. 206: Alan Vanneman reproduced with permission of Perseus Books. p. 221: quotation by Jean Anouilh from *Cécile, ou L'école des pères*, produced by Comédie des Champs-Elysées, 1949, published by Editions de la Table Ronde, 1954, translation by Luce Klein and Arthur Klein published as *Cécile, or The School for Fathers* in *From the Modern Repertoire: Series Three*, edited by Eric Bentley, Indiana University Press, 1956, reprinted with permission of Indiana University Press.

This English-language edition
© Flammarion, S.A., Paris, 2012

editions.flammarion.com

12 13 14   3 2 1

ISBN: 978-2-08-020128-7

Dépôt légal: 09/2012